HUMAN WORKS, ABSENT WORDS

Law, Man, and God
in Some Classical Philosophers

Christopher Berry Gray

University Press of America,® Inc.
Lanham · Boulder · New York · Toronto · Plymouth, UK

4501 Forbes Boulevard
Suite 200
Lanham, Maryland 20706
UPA Acquisitions Department (301) 459-3366

10 Thornbury Road
Plymouth PL6 7PP
United Kingdom

Printed in the United States of America
British Library Cataloging in Publication Information Available

Library of Congress Control Number: 2013952516
ISBN: 978-0-7618-5920-8 (clothbound : alk. paper)
eISBN: 978-0-7618-5921-5

This book is dedicated to my wife Kathleen Gray
whose support was indispensible.

CONTENTS

	Preface	vii
	Acknowledgements	ix
1	*Phaedo*'s Trivia	1
2	*Paideia, Schole, Paidia:* Then and Now	19
3	Finality's Flameout	25
4	External Goods and Contemplation in Aristotle	29
5	Aristotle's Text on Justice	34
6	Freedom and Necessity in St. Anselm's *Cur Deus Homo*	42
7	Bonaventure's Proof of Trinity	54
8	Civil Obligation in Bonaventure and 20th Century Anarchists	72
9	Specification of Norm in the Jurisprudences of Aquinas, Austin and Kelsen	81
10	Ockham on Trusts	93
11	Las Casas' Medieval Ideology	108

PREFACE

Classical philosophy never fails to refresh by its robust realism. The reality it affirms and then fortifies is presence of world to itself and thus to the knower. This confidence lets the classical philosopher and in turn the modern put to work techniques of appreciation that, when set onto modern philosophemes, can render only a shambles of constructivity. Interpretation based in the power of language, when grown in classic soil, handles virtuality as the reliable power it is, instead of making it a vapid substitution.

The varieties of classical thought canvass numerous idealist positions as well as subjectivist theories, to be sure. But in these the recognition of reality persists, however perspectivally diminished. This makes it possible for human and divine, for freedom and law to cohabit without fear of collapsing into piles of speculative shards. The human is the full-bodied person whose carnality and godliness is interpreted along with its mentality into the expressions that its philosophy voices. Talk by and of human and deity mutually implicate each other. Individual and society no less interdefine, so that to speak a philosophy of law is to speak equally the principles of human freedom.

The studies of Plato, Aristotle and Anselm outline concern for semiosis of a peircean style more visibly. But that extends into all the chapters through saussurean stress on the reality of absence and negation, what is unsaid as well as what is said. More recently famed as marginality, the distant bond to full knowledge is what Plato's charming of misology mediates us toward. This finality, the absent goal presented before us, allows Aristotle both to implant earthy contemplation in leisure, and grind it into a more useable justice. For Anselm temporal distance founds the contingent will in being with the existential firmness that elsewhere lets dialectic ground godhead for this partisan of revived Lombard jurisprudence.

The real kinship of will to law lofts Bonaventure's philosophy of imagery, not only up to the rarities of triunity, but down to the pedestrian features of penal law. Everywhere the present imports the absent. No less do Ockham and Las Casas ride the vehicle of imagery past the confines of duties and property, on into rights and trust; and past enslavement in ethnicity, biology as destiny, into the equality of rights bearers. Release from the restrictive positivity of modern avatars is the way in which Aquinas' specification of legal norm manifests the sinuous presence of non-being as virtual identity for the subject of law.

Religious folk may see all this as the reality of redemption already achieved, ever panting to be appropriated and made actual by its beneficiaries. As philosophers we see absence and mediation as the structure of being, the world's and ours, always present and always confounding both the sheer positivity of a parmenidean Kant as much as the sheer negativity of a heraclitean Nietzsche.

And through it all the reader, the thinker of classical texts, is engaged. She stands outside the subject even less than the reader of moderns. For while today we construct ourselves in constructing the texts which construct our world, then the meaning of god, man and world are mutually constructive; so that we invoke those other agencies of our existence upon our formation when we exercise ours upon them.

My gratitude to the late Thomas Prufer, Professor of Philosophy at The Catholic University of America in Washington DC, remains untarnished fifty years after he opened several of these avenues to me, with his colleagues Robert Sokolowski and John Smolko.

ACKNOWLEDGEMENTS

Versions or portions of several of the following chapters have appeared in other publications: Ch. 2 in *Philosophy of Man at Recreation and Leisure*, C.B. Gray (New York: Peter Lang, 2007), Appendix; Ch. 5 in *Texts* (New York: Fordham, 1999) 163-170; Ch. 6 in *Franciscan Studies* 36 (1976) 177-191; Ch. 7 in *American Catholic Philosophical Quarterly* 67 (1993) 201-217; Ch. 8 in *American Catholic Philosophical Quarterly* 85 (2011) 203-212; Ch. 9 in *Aquinas* 23 (1980) 79-92; Ch. 10 in *Franciscan Studies* 46 (1986) 143-159; Ch. 11 in *Les philosophies morales et politiques au Moyen-Age/ Moral and Political Philosophies of the Middle Ages*, ed. B. Carlos Bazan, E. Andujar, L. G. Sbrocci (Ottawa: Legas, 1995), and in Spanish in *Patristica et Mediaevalia* 14 (1993) 3.

Not all of these require permissions for republication; but, where they do, the permissions have been obtained.

CHAPTER ONE

PHAEDO'S TRIVIA

This study remains at the point of origin for Plato's dialogues, Socrates' death in the *Phaedo*, and tries to let the sense of misology (89d) show through. Plato builds his dialogue up to and down from this text as almost a numerical center of the lines. Within this horizon, his proofs for the immortality of discoursing manhood are made as certain as their mythic counterparts.

Many points in this study would seem unimportant to students of the *Phaedo*. But in order to interpret a text it is essential to focus upon context, and the *trivium* is the classical way to do this. We attend to how the speech of the author-speaker is related to hearer (rhetoric). We observe at what point the words make contact with their referents (logic). We estimate where these words fit at just this point among the possibilities for speaking, whether actualized or not (grammar). This final focus is employed too briefly at start and finish, lest an already overlong study become impossibly diffuse in secondary and historical references.

THE "DEATH DIALOGUES" ARE MUTUALLY CONSISTENT REGARDING THE LAW: GRAMMAR[1]

Outside the court Euthyphro had joined Socrates in seeking the holy, for only this will let one go before the law conscientiously and respect the city. But Euthyphro breaks off the search for universals—"no time right now"—and we are left to answer out of the particular case of Socrates.

His answer, however, is confusing. There is violation of the law required by the very foundations of law in the *Apology*. Then there is obedience to the law even in its most literal form just as strongly demanded on the same or perhaps even deeper grounds in the *Crito*. But finally there is the reconciliation of the two apparent contradictories by the human precondition for both in the *Phaedo*.

The lack of effrontery and impudence (*Apology* 38d) which so offends the jurors is that Socrates would rather obey God than man (29d), violating the words of law at their basic source in the lawmaking assembly. The prisoner's friend can save him from the very injustice of the lower law he had fought in court, but the positive law now takes on the same sanctity as did the god at the trial, Socrates felt compelled to reject the legal words in court, now he must stand for their inviolability.

Laws are words which establish the possibility for words. But the words of law as physical entities or even as meaningful signs cannot do this. Article x, section y, paragraph z are the legal words; but the word of law is not identified with these, for they are not the word-permitting law which Socrates homages but are only its mode of presence. The ultimate responsibility before law does not appeal to that law as the final location of responsibility; if it were not that *pacta sunt servanda* before legal words, it would not be that way after words, either. On the other hand, that responsibility is not a responsibility to anything until the law exists as written words; there is no object for the responsibility. Once laws are established there is the responsibility towards them, but not because of them. Law is the final word, but it says nothing for itself. It does not speak of law but only of what is not law, of events judged legally to exist.

The only responsibility prior to law is to truth, for Socrates. But for the pious *man* who is no heaven-stormer, truth is not totally presented. The only way truth is available is in contrast to what is, by a contrast to what it is not, i.e., to opinion. Truth is available only in opinion; opinion is possible only where law makes it possible. Responsibility to law, then, is responsibility to truth. It is not what is in law that is sacred, but rather that law is there. To desert law is to desert truth by deserting the location of truth's possibility, opinionated speech made possible by law.

Discourse is the center of humanness; its locus is in political existence; politics is a matter of constitutional law. Thus does Socrates the rebel of the *Apology* come to terms with Socrates the slave of the *Crito*. The *Phaedo* now penetrates the nature of such speech, as the swan song for Socrates to sing.

WE ARE INVOLVED BY BEING ADDRESSED ABOUT MISOLOGY: RHETORIC

The men who speak in the *Phaedo* are recalled as Socrates and his friends; most memorable among these are Socrates and the argumentative Simmias and Cebes. But the namesake of the dialogue appears among the disciples only at the precise middle of the dialogue (89b–d), where he is engaged by Socrates in the warning against misology. Phaedo does appear at other points, not in dialogue with Socrates but with Echecrates, telling him of the deathbed discourse. These secondary interchanges are found at two pairs of points, at the very beginning and end of the dialogue (57a and 117b), and again in the middle of the dialogue (88d and 102a) where they frame the central interchange between Phaedo and Socrates. Only between the first and second Phaedo-Echecrates exchanges (59d–88d), and again between their third and fourth (102b–117b), does Socrates discourse with the other friends. These give Socrates an entrance and an exit; the first discourse begins in his absence outside the jail, and the second ends in his absence after the execution.

The final figures active in the dialogue are Plato and ourselves. Xanthippe and the jailor precede the first discourse and follow the last. Evenus, fresh from his role in the *Apology* as sophist and now the poet promoting Socrates' popularization of philosophy in dialogic song, is given a role as are the various heroes we shall meet further on; but only Plato and we are important more for being absent than present. We are too important to be overlooked as the obvious reader and writer[2]; instead we are given frank epiphanies as absent partners, as "anyone hearing this" (70c) and as "Plato, I believe, was ill" (59b). Plato and we stand external to, and so present to the whole dialogue and each of its parts; for the sake of symmetry our involvement can be viewed, however, as temporally outside of the dialogue, before and after the Phaedo-Echecrates boundaries.

This rhetorical arrangement is accurate for both spatial and temporal presence, and also for their bodily contact. Plato and we are most distant from the events and from each other in all senses, Phaedo and Echecrates are less so; Socrates and the disciples are quite close, while Phaedo and Socrates are at the very heart and also are the only ones who exchange bodily caresses. Phaedo narrates because he is the heart, not the ostensible Simmias and Cebes. Each set radiates outward the meanings and serves as the medium for the other's approach: Socrates to Phaedo, to the disciples, to Echecrates, to Plato, to us. Because each carries the message in the same way it was delivered—it is almost a commonplace that this medium is Socrates' message—the successive dialogue partners involve the outsiders just as intimately as the originals. Each partner serves to broaden the involvement and to resist spectating; to grasp the message, one must already have begun to practice its recommendations. As in Pythagoras' response to the king, not those who play sports and hawk wares are most "into" the Grecian games, but those who attend them, religiously. Thus each engages the next, right down to ourselves; this study is our response. Socrates and company do not involve us immediately; on the contrary, the whole thrust is toward mediation, even for those within the cell. But he does involve us inexcusably, by the rhetorical devices mediating us towards philosophy.

This rhetoric of voice and address has an hourglass form: from us to Plato, to Echecrates, the disciples and Phaedo, to Socrates and the living presence of philosophy, back out to Socrates, Phaedo, the friends and Echecrates, to Plato and to us. The only bulges in the hourglass are the brief Phaedo-Echecrates interjections framing the Phaedo-Socrates center of misology. The hourglass funnels in toward this point, and thus makes it possible authentically to expand back out from it. Even the bulges serve this end, for Phaedo and Echecrates interrupt the tale here to express anguish and then relief over the Socratic crux, too passionate simply to stand and listen. And since one of them, Phaedo, is within that crux, he brings it out directly into the external world of discourse, a privileged while in principle impossible entry through a different dimension.

The Dialogue's Referent is the Act of Speaking the Dialogue: Logic

Rhetorical structure points toward the key interchange, but does not say what it is about. Only a study of what is said in the dialogue will satisfy the anticipations aroused by the rhetoric. The same approach will be used here as in approaching the rhetoric; we will scan the succession of contexts for discussion defined by the objects of discussion, and then look at the beginning-to-end sequence in detail.

The *Phaedo* rewards study with an hourglass-shaped logical structure which centers upon the very same locus as the rhetoric, namely the misology crux, but a structure whose symmetry tells us different information than does the rhetoric. The dialogue both begins and ends in a religious context: the sacrificial ship's ritual voyage in memory of Theseus has given stay of execution to Socrates (58a); and the demand for payment of a cock to Aesculapius is preceded by covering of the face, by prayer, attempted libation, all before the sun sets and after a purifying bath, both contrary to the customs of victims who dine into the night and leave the bath for their undertakers (116–117). The religious context, just as the person Phaedo and for the same reason, penetrates also into the heart of the misology discourse, where the hero Hercules is invoked.

Just inside this sacrificial frame is a dimension fit to be characterized as fabulous. Socrates initiates discussion by reference to Aesop (60c), and ends it with the trip through Hades and earth (107d). These lead into and are led into by, respectively, encouragements to care for the soul (61c, 1107b), the first at length and the second a brief ferverino to draw the preceding arguments to a head. Inside of these, it is the arguments for immortality of soul which form the traditional focus upon the *Phaedo*; and traditionally the two main routes they pursue are by the arguments from opposites and from forms. However, only the first such argumentation treats the proofs in this order (70a), while the second returns to them in reverse orders looking first to the argument from forms and only then the argument from opposites (102b).

It is following these arguments that Simmias and Cebes pose their devastating objections (85a), which elicit instantaneous answers from Socrates (92a). It is the havoc wreaked upon the company by these objections of the lyre's harmony and the tailor's coats which require Socrates first to reassure them in the very middle of the dialogue (89d) about the value of argument, before going on to pointed answers.

The way to read the meaning of such a structure will be nailed down from internal evidence but at this point the following might be suggested. The points outside the dialogue, of Plato and ourselves, are the mindless natural attitude of concern with things other than the death of Socrates. We are mediated out of and back into this by the conventional rituals of religion. From this and back to this lead the poet's work of fables which exercise speech in a conventional but highly self-conscious and self-controlled manner. But it is care of the soul, of the personal identity and dignity, which the first fable suggests and which elicits the second. To take this up responsibly, one must be assured it is not futile; this is the function of the arguments for immortality. And for any argument to be so effective, each person must be aware of his identity as inescapably inserted into a speech community and active within it, which the central misology text urges. What we shall look for in a detailed study of the words of the *Phaedo* are literal and figurative enunciations of the identity between human and dialogue, as well as its implications.

The rhetorical and logical structures take this form, whose identifying numbers and letters will be used to locate discussions from here on in the text.

Rhetorical Structure	Logical Structure
A. Plato & us	
B. Phaedo & Echecrates 57a	1. religious context: Theseus 58a
C. Socrates & friends 59a	2. fabulous context: Aesop 60c
	3. care of the soul 61a
	4. arguments: opposites; forms 70a
	5. objections: harmony; durability 85a
D. Phaedo & Echecrates 88d	
E. Socrates & Phaedo 89b*	6. misology 89d
F. Phaedo & Echecrates 102a	
G. Socrates & friends 102b	7. answers: evil; biography 92a
	8. arguments: evil; opposites 102b
	9. care of the soul 107b
	10. fabulous context: Hades 107d
	11. religious: Aesculapius 116a
H. Phaedo & Echecrates 117b	
I. Plato & us	

1B

The dialogue opens with Phaedo at pains to confirm his status as a witness to his own involvement. Severity of questioning determines the exact circumstances of place, time, setting, personnel and reasons; the courtroom situation is restored, and the scene is set for Socrates' prison defence to excel over his courtroom defence. One is reminded of the third chapter of Luke, the evangelist who is also at pains to give exact reference points of genealogy and reign to pinpoint historically the mission of Jesus.

Socrates' execution is so long delayed after his condemnation because of the mission to Delos. This mission not only sets the sacrificial scene, as noted above, but provides a continuing reference point throughout the entire dialogue, as Socrates' and others' identity is fixed and their words or actions interpreted by holding up the personage related to this mission at that point. Before it is through, some half-dozen figures will be related to it.

But the interpretation begins even before the *Phaedo* commences. Euthyphro had been inveigled before the case was heard to declare that Socrates made his arguments walk about like Daedelus' automatons. Socrates acknowledges this skill, but unwillingly, since it is his partner's claims that are unstable and he just sets loose their own wandering. However, he finds the source of his skill in the fact that Daedelus was the founder of his line (llcd).

Daedelus, it is recalled, was the architect of the Labyrinth wherein, to test its insolubility, he is stranded by Minos of Crete, his employer. Equally clever at aerodynamics, he and his son fly out but meet tragedy when Icarus lofts too near the source of light and, like Oedipus, plummets from his height of hubris. Socrates' task is in part to keep his progeny from this fate, to shield them by teaching them to mediate the light through each other and attain learned ignorance.

Daedulus' Labyrinth is the scene for Theseus' adventure, which Socrates' garlanded ship commemorates. In the Labyrinth the king of Crete has imprisoned the Minotaur, a savage half-man, half-bull, sated only by the slaughter of seven maidens and youths demanded yearly by Crete from vassal Athens. Theseus, son of the king of Athens, undertakes to end the tribute and the Minotaur, which he does after infatuating the Cretan princess Ariadne into revealing that he can unroll thread from the entrance and retrace it to the exit. In his elation at victory he forgets to change the ship's black sail for white upon return, and King Aegeus suicides over his son's presumed death because the prearranged sign was not given.

Socrates is to fill many roles here. As savior of Athens' youth from the toils of custom and contradictory red tape, he still must die upon the ship's return. Death need be only a symbolic sacrifice thereafter because Socrates offers unconcern over physical death to those who are led out of the maze of immediacy. To collect the loose ends dangling out of recollection and to follow them back out is the route. His success is incomplete, however, and we shall see the figure carried out later in Hercules to show why.

2C

While nothing gives more pleasure than recalling the memory of Socrates (58d), the master has warned it will be bitter; for just as Phaedo experienced the most peculiar combination of pleasure and pain with Socrates on death row (59a), so the master commences with an Aesop-like fable regarding the same. And since he frankly announces that his mission is now to go beyond philosophy and sing its lines more imaginatively (60e), he has given fair warning of what Plato's composition upon opposites can be expected to be, and what the opposition of philosophy to the whole pleasure and pain context means.

Since it is the god who has stayed execution, and since this dialogue is the more convincing formal defence against the charges at his trial (63b) due now to his accusers' willingness to participate, Socrates is in the context of the citizenry as a whole and must sweeten the lip of his cup in ways lacking at the trial. This hymn to Apollo (61b), whose servant Socrates is and whose swan song he here sings (85b), to whose son he offers his sacrifice (118a), must honor Apollo as god not only of truth but of creative imagination. So the high and difficult doctrine regarding humans' station in the world, as in a guardhouse, invoked in the *Apology* monologue (28e), will be here played down (62b) in favor of comfort from the thought of good masters (63c). What remains is service, but its reward is stressed. Socrates' dialogue is in the context not of a deontological metaphysics but of a eudaimonological; even though the pleasure and pain context is explicitly inveighed, this is still what the fable is concerned with, even in its most abstract reaches regarding the opposites.

3C

Of course, at this point Socrates' feet are up in the air and not .firmly planted (60a). But he soon begins to chant the fable of interrelationship in earnest and comes back to earth, Thus he remains with feet on the ground (61c) until he lives out the fable by dying, feet up but weighed down and overcome by the gravity of dealing with earthly things (117a). A man's sincerity even over the highest things to be shared still verges upon the self-important and insolent ignorance whose fatal consequences he must anticipate and accept.

The companions are to occupy the time that they are in the daylight, their life, with imagining their afterlife; the birth to death gap is filled with questions of birth and death. There is. really nothing else to do (61e), for all their actions ready them inexorably for whatever future condition they make for themselves. Discourse on this sole subject has only one sole criterion, that life is better than death (62a). Socrates stresses both that this is the only dogma and that his knowledge of it is hearsay. If we add the claim of the *Apology* that the unexamined life is not worth living, then the life to be preserved from death is that life of dialogue. The jailor recognizes this by informing the party, in effect, that talking makes it difficult to die. (63d). If the philosopher's life is a continual dying, and this life is the only worthwhile one, and if finally one must await the services of another in bringing himself unto death (62a), then it becomes clear just what life is later claimed to be immortal and also how that immortality is to be earned, not just acknowledged.

If the philosopher seeks explanation by "what is better", as the autobiography further on claims, and if the sole dogma is that life is better than death, then how could the philosopher find any explanation for death other than in terms of a contribution towards continuing life? How could he find death in death, how could he find anything there but philosophic immortality, the better?[3]

For Socrates to die, philosophically, he needs the service of others, who in turn need us readers; only in such appearance can courage and wisdom in death be present. Socrates is not arguing that no one need fear death, but only one who has been busy about philosophy (63e). That is to say, himself. Now, at least, Socrates could not be seen as the busybody with his head in *The Clouds* (70c), for his inquiry into afterlife is immediate to him. So his argument about afterlife regards his own afterlife, and only secondarily states that the philosopher need not fear death, and only very remotely if at all that all do in fact survive—which hardly remedies the fear of everyone, good and evil alike. This is an appeal for conversion, not a declaration of dogma on a par with the sole dogma. This is why his courage before death is his answer to the jury; it is not incorrigibility nor intractability, but concern and conviction. In a philosopher this reproves condemnation for practicing philosophy. For Socrates has a standing before the justice of eternity only because of his practice of philosophy, for which he was condemned. Yet it is this legal standing which allows him to prove his point by courage out of wisdom. Because his speaking now is one with his speaking before, it makes the other authoritative too.

So courage and self-control are contradictory for everyone else, who define them in terms of their opposites, fear and intemperance (68d). The only route to consistency is to separate from the body; this is what death is, nothing more and nothing less (64c,67d), But, as he shall argue, opposites do generate one another; and, even more, philosophy is being generated in the opposition of Socrates and his interlocutors. So the only event which could truly be death would be separation from the body of interlocutors, and this is the death Socrates knows is not terminal for the body. The irony of the ascesis Socrates describes as the way of saying what he means is too patent to be overlooked. While body makes knowledge inaccurate we know this fact only because the poets have told our ears that our ears are inaccurate (65b), the toils of the liar paradox. If pure thought is possible regarding pure objects only apart from body (65e–66a), then what is Socrates doing wasting his time pursuing it here with others? For his teaching is not the silence of *zazen*. As Socrates forthrightly tells them, indeed there is for the philosophical life an allegorical meaning in religious initiation into afterlife (69c), but his own philosophical allegory for what the philosophical life is needs equal unravelling, which we are engaged in here.[4]

4C

The hypothetical character of the argumentation proper is made explicit from its start. Socrates begins the inquiry by noting that it is a "point of view" (*skepsometha tede pe*) (70c). Whether souls exist in another world is the way to ask whether souls continue to exist at all. How could there be a coherent, i.e. besouled, world different from ours? Continued existence is inconceivable without a world like this one, only better.

The legends say there is one, whose recollection permits knowledge of this present world. Without it, entropy would reduce all to stasis (72be), i.e., the negative of any two opposites would win out and end the opposition (71e). There is nothing particularly human or soul-related about this event, for it is a mechanism of cosmic categories, although later (79b) the criterion for all such events is made their availability to the kind of knowledge belonging to human persons. It is interesting that opposites meet, that the cosmic self-sufficiency which earlier threatened a Heraclitean universe in fact dooms us to a Parmenidean one.

Plato has made us absent parties participate in Socrates' present; now with the theory of recollection he makes present things participate through our own past in forms which are not so much absent as they are only approachable. Again, the closeness between discourse and object is not a frill but is an agency for accomplishing what is said. Simmias asks Socrates to recollect for him the theory of recollection (73a); and just so we won't overlook this, he then asks him for help to do what they are talking about (73b). When this is fortified by other passages to the same effect, as where it is urged that an argument about harmony is hardly the place for discord in the argument (92c), it is unmistakably clear that the argument itself is the locus of what the argument concerns, namely, the absolutes or forms recollected, i.e., harmonized, and giving immortality.

Problems arise, however, in the kinship the knower must have to the known. When do we lose knowledge (76d), is a legitimate problem if the soul is absolute by its kinship to ideas. Again, pleasure and pain is the context abhorred for the philosopher yet the philosophical heaven and hell are described in terms of them (81–82 , esp. 83c). In addition, if evil (but immortal) human souls go next to animals, why on the next round are the souls associated with persons the only immortal souls, rather than those of animals, too? Again, if anyone can explain the questions of knowledge because all can recall the forms, how are they recalled by those evil people who never return to the true earth to experience forms, but are flushed around in the underworld rivers? It seems that only the philosopher could have seen them, so only he can answer the questions posed; and so he can answer them only to other philosophers. Finally, if body is mortal and if some souls do not lose attachment to body, then immortality must be the end not of all, but only of philosophers. That is, immortality is contingent upon action, not necessitated by nature.

The way out of the problem is that recollection can be brought about by reminders quite different from what they remind one of (74c). Likeness to ideas is what proves immortality but this likeness is not a quality of nature, given in full. Instead, likeness and so immortality is a quality of action, such that we bring about, or do not bring about, the immortality Socrates argues about.

So Socrates agrees with Simmias that there are flaws, and that what he said about native immortality is still open to doubt (84c), such as that souls' active nature may cease with the activity, or be worn out in the long run of action. Nonetheless, the topic must be pursued, even if without certainty, because it is important (85cd). Maybe at best one can only find a theory to ride, if not facts, if there is no revelation available (85od). Whichever, the story of immortality needs to be chanted over and over, as to a child, to calm not so much his mind as his imagination. That is, in lieu of a solid proof, one must apply an appealing proof, as a spell to charm fears away, so that one will then act confidently in a way that will ensure the immortality he thought at first was secured, until he no longer needs the crutch of false belief to foster his true behavior, behavior which makes his belief come true.[5] Even after the proofs are given, one must spin them out until they convince.

The only dogma is that life is better than death. Any other belief will be taken seriously and at face value only to the extent it supports this. Arguments on forms and opposites convince some, while descriptions of afterworlds do others; but the criterion of either is this instrumental role. Not only the endless stasis of Anaxagoras (72c) must be avoided, but also the endless change of Penelope (84a). Humans must be able to earn and end their destinies, not arrogantly but still once and for all; that destiny is unending depth of truth.

6E

Humans' bodily presence at the center of meaning is what the entry into the misology crux involves us in all too frankly. When Socrates fondles Phaedo's curls after Cebes and Simmias attack the arguments, he tells Phaedo to go into mourning right now and not after the execution, for the real death that is imminent is that of argument and not that of Socrates (89b). Or better: Socrates' real death to mourn is the death of his argument; the death of the real Socrates is the death of his argument. The identity of the Socrates whose immortality has been at issue is the *logos*, the argument. As long as the argument lives, so does the man. Such a treasure is more precious than any golden fleece sought by the consecrated Argives, but can be grasped only by turning the dragon's brood upon each other in verbal tension. Theseus' presence on that mission is not to be overlooked; nor the fact that the ubiquitous Medea follows the fleece back with Jason, and thereafter flees to wed Aegeus, Theseus' father, whom she later leads to make an attempt on his son's life. We shall see another wicked stepmother later; but for now Phaedo is being told that even if the counterargument is crushed, and argument is reappreciated, the attached price to pay for keeping his hirsute good looks is that he escape tragedy at best by a hairsbreadth.

The Hercules reference (89c) clarifies this point. Theseus' cousin though Zeus and the younger hero's model, Hercules takes as his second labor to slay the Hydra. Since its monstrous nine heads reincarnate by growing back, he brings along his nephew Iolaus to brand and cauterize the stumps as he lops off the heads. But the operation is not a complete success, for the ninth head is immortal and can only be buried beneath a huge rock. The need for the partner is the intransigent flaw that keeps our hero honest. The soul's immortality is reached through pressing the forms and their opposition, and defeat of the counterarguments is carried off in cooperation. But the dialogue partner's indispensable presence as other and as fleshly stands as a constant rebuke to what is being said by the two. All that can be done with it is to cover it over until it no longer is seen as a counterargument to immortality, but as a proof of that. For it is the incompletion of the dogma of immortality which keeps speech immortal; if it is impossible for man to complete or exhaust it, then never can the task be finished off.[6] The discourser can never fully subsume his own position; immortality can never become itself a quality or form, but.solely the lived existence which keeps getting in its own way. It matters little who is Hercules and who is Iolaus in the interchange, for it is their sheer duality that is tragic.

The Theban boys, Simmias and Cebes, have required Socrates' labor to meet their objections that the lyre loses its harmony and the tailor finally dies off before his last coat. Socrates takes the opportunity to refer their arguments back respectively to Harmonia and Cadmus, founders of Thebes, the cursed house of Oedipus, and the maternal ancestors of Theseus the hero of Athens (95a). There is obvious play upon the Lady Harmonia; the allusion to Cadmus is less obvious, whose crop of girt warriors (the same seed who plagued Jason) found his city instead of all killing each other, and who introduced to Greece his native Phoenician alphabet and thus to Socrates the rationality that the Theban offspring enforce.

But the focus is set upon Oedipus. More even than Daedelus, Theseus and Hercules, the success of his venture carries a sting. His tragic flaw is the wish for direct exposure to the truth. But, as before an eclipse, some medium is needed lest one be blinded instead of enlightened (99e). So one must not boast about the argument's success, lest some misfortune befall it (95b). The boys do not yet recognize that their very presence disproves the best proof Socrates can offer for the conclusion they relish, while proving the conclusion he is arguing. Nor could they accept this. They must be led towards the acceptance that they are wise only if they know they are not wise, even if the passage towards it must obscure the meaning which Socrates openly, and thus invisibly, moves now toward giving it.

The clue lies in the open comparison Socrates makes, which in a word comes down to this: misology and misanthropy are the same thing (89d). The positive statement of the same is that *logos* and *anthropos* are the same thing; and the consequence is that the immortality of humans is equivalent to the immortality of argument. This is the Hydra's immortal head; there is none of the impersonal, value-neutral reason which is being sought, but only the ordered speech of men. One cannot expect to finish it, one can reject as beneath consideration nothing that another says. Thus one can never be scandalized at the failure to reach the impossible dream, one can never be put off at the failure of any particular argument. Ordered speech is immortal, the attempt to order speech is immortal. The confirmation that it is embodied reason who is the object of this interchange occurs when Socrates speaks frankly of the resemblance between arguments and human beings (90b).

The fault lies not in human existence but in human beings who rush in where Socrates, at least, fears to tread. This is what Socrates is providing these disciples, a preparation for such demystification, an immunization in much the same way as social scientists geld their students' social fury, by showing that all existence falls along some normal curve of distribution (89e–90a) and that socialized reality is mediocre. The pedagogical difference is that Socrates goes on to offer the hope which they cannot say, by using the vehicle of language to show it.

For wisdom does not lie in knowing that nothing is stable or sure; that would be to shift the blame to the reason, not the reasoner, and then one would miss even what knowledge is possible. One must rather keep a frustrated faith in argument and in humans, so that if knowledge is possible then one is ready for it (90cd). This is closer to the meaning of Socrates' claim at his trial that he is wise because he knows he is not wise; it is the direct reverse of any skepticism, neither the anarchism of Heraclitus and Penelope nor the arch-conservatism of Parmenides and Anaxagoras. It is the true meaning, also, of the sole dogma that life is better than death, for faith is the only means of properly human survival while surrender is death. One cannot come back from the dead when that death is not just individual death, but the very death of the absolute.

This is the philosophical piety that answers Euthyphro and with which Socrates concludes his Apologia, that only God knows if death is an evil and so one is impious if he bases action upon the presumption that it is evil. This is the hubris of presuming to know the unknowable. Instead, Socrates now repels Aristophanes' mockery, for he is only trying to provide sufficient conviction for himself alone to remain pious (91a). The only proof of his claim to wisdom, on this basis, then, can be argument by retrorsion, not the ostensible proofs by forms and opposites. So, although he soothes his friends with the useful truth that will soon pass if false (91b), he immediately urges them back to the attack, lest the gadfly's sting endure when he no longer does (91c). For even if his claim to unending reason is false, it will endure endlessly infecting them. Thus strongly grows his argument, that the very defeat of the arguments for it in fact confirm it, not infirm it.

7F

We are now on the way out of this profound depth of despair and hope over reason, back toward the rippling natural attitude. Socrates continues by detailing just how his encouragement to philosophical faith is to be effected, how we must not let it enter our minds that there may be no validity to argument. First one must stick to a worthy hypothesis which permits such a faith, as to no other theory (92a). For this reason, such a hypothesis has more claim on belief than does any analogy more appealing at first sight (92d). For example, since no soul can be any more or less a soul than another (93d) and since at all costs one must preserve the possibility for evil (93c, 94b) and thereby the possibility for men and so arguments to fail without being disqualified, one will have to give up attunement and hold to recollection. We have already seen the reference to the parallel attunements of argument, arguers and argued; that is, the referent of what is said here is the very saying of it. The disposition of the analogy is that attunement follows the components while soul directs them (94c).

Socrates continues to describe what theory consists of as he tries to pull the many teeth of the second objection. To show that embodied reason is not merely long-lived but immortal (95c) requires reflection upon a life lived through, for example Socrates' autobiography; it proves nothing, but it may show something (95e–96a). One can test whether he is ready to begin distinguishing causes from conditions, as Socrates certainly is now faced with flight or right (99ab), as in the *Crito*. His own makeshift and muddling way (99d, 97b) for avoiding excessive exposure to truth is to place a filter to both separate and join him to the truth. Not that any other way of knowing is available which would not involve such medium, only that this is the most fundamentalist method: he can cling through change to the old rugged theory in a way he could not do to fact. Agreement or disagreement with the theory which looks soundest is the criterion for acceptance or rejection (99e–100a). Dismiss all refinements, just hold to the hypothesis, dismiss any challenges to that hypothesis, but for oneself justify the hypothesis by clutching whatever more ultimate one will support the first. Do not assume that any unpleasant consequences of the principle constitute a critique of it (191c–e).

Small wonder Socrates finds this method foolish and vacant of detail (100d), and smiles over how artificial it sounds when applied (102d), despite the fact that it is the safest way and all others are confusing (100d). Yet this is just the suggestion which convinces Simmias and Cebes, and thereafter Phaedo and Echecrates (102a). That is to say, this fundamentalism supports the basic dogma by driving all away from misology, and that is sufficient to justify it. Socrates has led them to do what he describes, without them ever noting the fact that it is the mere description of a possibility which has done this real work.

8G

Once this is indelibly established, Socrates can take the luxury of making the answer more sophisticated, in place of the safe but ingenuous answer (105bc), even at the price now of altering radically what had been said in the safer discourse. After all, he is saying all this only to get them to share his point of view (102d) which, once achieved, he can mediate back toward reality. There had been shown no other way for a given object to exist than by participation in the reality peculiar to its appropriate universal (101c); and it had been laughable, to Cebes at least (101b), that this view could be supported by such nonsense as the autological and heterological features of tallness and shortness (101a). Now, however, Socrates moves not only from saying that opposite things come from opposite things to saying that the form of the opposite can never become opposite to itself (103b), but also from here to saying that opposite forms cannot face one another's approach, and thence that things partaking of opposite forms cannot abide each other (104c). That is, while the living come from the dead, the soul partaking of life is simply displaced by the death partaking of mortality.

The only "sharing" or "participating" which can be done is the participation of persons in personal relations and activity; any other usage is metaphorical. Either this is true, or its reverse is, namely, that personal participation is mere metaphor. The pointers Socrates has given us until now would suggest the first.

If there is no way something can come into being but by participating in the reality peculiar to its appropriate universal (101c), and since the reality peculiar to man is that of ordered speech, embodied reason, then man has reality through partaking of dialogue. And he continues existence on the same basis. As long as speech lasts, man lasts, especially the philosopher whose life is that of ordered speech.

To harmonize the claims that opposites are both in a participant in order to characterize him in relatively opposite ways (191a), and that something attached to one opposite cannot be characterized in any way by the other (105ab), we must continue in the same context. As Socrates is stressing, the refusal of misology implies that it is not indifferent which of two contradictories are true; both cannot be, and these are the incompatible opposites themselves, as well as the opposition between misology and philosophy. Instead, the opposites which do generate each other and characterize each other are the opponents in dialogue taking up those incompatible positions. For the survival of man, the possibility of knowledge, these contradictories must be mediated through instances, the discussants, who do find each other mutually compatible and coexistent. The only opposition which could not be so mediated and shielded from the harsh light of real contradiction is that between misology and philosophy. But Socrates' discussion here is living proof of the non-ultimacy of that opposition, since there is no reality to the former pole. The first can comprehend neither itself nor the other, while the second can comprehend .itself, even if not the other. This is the only approach of opposites where courage might fail (103d), but Socrates has just pulled the teeth of this monster, and he can move on to death with courage.

9G

We can feel the argument's power, but still have misgivings over it both from the weakness of our knowing powers and from the elusiveness of the subject, along with Simmias (107a). But all one can do is to go over it again (105b), since this is all that human knowing is capable of; to expect more is impiety, losing not only what was anticipated but even what we have (107b).

10G

Among the several forms to set this repetitious study is the forthrightly imaginative. While it is frankly a matter of belief and hearsay (109de), there is no degeneracy in doing this, since we now know that theory is no less embedded into images than is fact (100a). It is quite possible for an imaginative tale to show the reality (110b), at least at the proper moment for it (110b). While not fact, nor even reasonable, its criterion of truth is that it agrees with what is known to be true, and has the end of promoting it (114d). To speak in a mythically inaccurate way, even informally, is bad for the soul (115e).

The main feature of the trip to the real heaven and earth is that there are many choices to be made and a guide or companion is needed; this surely accommodates the dialogue partner Socrates has made central to personhood. The earth to be negotiated must be explained in accord with Socrates' final criterion of cosmology: that it explains by what is best (97cd). Thus the earth is self-supporting, a homeostatic balance of opposite forces (108e–109a); this is what Socrates has been trying to argue for the human condition throughout. Its substances are unmixed, its underworld rivers do not mingle, any more than do the opposites, any more than do the lifestyles or virtues necessitated by proximity to respective opposites. All the descriptions make clear that the state of the separated soul on the true earth is the very state of the imprisoned soul now, namely, a bodily condition, but better or more bodily. Even though it is a tale, this is not an allegory like the tale of the *Republic*'s philosopher who crawls from the cave to the sunlight of the earth's surface; this is supposed to be narrative description of reality, even if not exactly. Accordingly, unlike the caveman, the earthman can never face the sun directly, without being blinded by excess of light (99e). Overall, the description places on the soul its own identity, not a borrowed splendor (114e). No more is it to be draped in forms than it is to be tricked out in wealth and pleasures. The opposites that have been so prominent are once again returned to their existential status in human intercourse.

This is Socrates' existence, too. To please him we must care for the soul, by philosophy as he described (115b). This Socrates to be pleased is he who marshals arguments, not the later speechless corpse (115ed). Socrates.is dead because he no longer speaks; his executioner's explanation is ludicrous in the light of Socrates' own cosmology, that Socrates will be dead because the poison will have reached his heart, rather than because he knew it best (118a).

The disciples say they will feel like orphans without him, yet those who will actually be Socrates' blood orphans are sent away by him (116ab); their father is not being lost while they continue, but rather they actively lose him and he actively parts from them in death, carrying to the end the reality of continuance sustained in the dialogue argument. While these children and his wife are sent away for shedding tears because they are hopelessly out of touch with what Socrates knows is happening, and as the jailor is found charming and generous to shed tears since no more can be expected of him although he has begun the climb in dialogue with Socrates (116d), the disciples are vigorously reprimanded. For if mere careless naming implies that the soul is mortal, and so corrupts the soul, what must such vigorous display do to turn their heart from the truth of death.

11G

The final command to Crito, symmetrical with his opening command to Crito, sums up Socrates' status in the dialog and in life, and the position of humans in existence according to the extension intended by the dialogue. Born of the god Apollo and reared by the half-horse Chiron, Aesculapius the medical hero restores Theseus' son Hippolytus from the curse of death laid on by his jealous stepmother and lover Phaedra. But instead of the customary rooster to stipend his service, Aesculapius is killed by Zeus' thunderbolt on the wish of Pluto, who has been cheated of his prey, to pay with his life for the patient's return to health. So is Socrates, both patient and physician, neither beast nor god but both at one, trying to save Athens' manhood from its best-intentioned polluters.

11H

It is not possible for the jailor to overlook Socrates' virtue; he is "noblest, gentlest and bravest" (116c: *gennaiotatos kai praotatos kai aristos*). But it is only those who have entered philosophy who can recognize true virtue. Phaedo can eulogize Socrates instead as "bravest, wisest and most upright" (118a: *aristos kai allos phronomotatos kai dikaiotatos*), taking up right where the jailor left off. The brave man is virtuous (*aristos*); but to move from the appearance of virtue in nobility and gentleness to its reality in wisdom and justice requires the movement through death in bravery. While the commonplace virtues will permit us to face one another peaceably, only taking advantage of this for dialogue will make us able to confirm these virtues in philosophical virtue.

ARGUMENTS FOR THIS SORT OF IMMORTALITY ARE VALID: GRAMMAR (2)

It is now possible to examine the relationship of the words of the dialogue to one another, that is, to perceive how well the point is proven. This can be done fairly rapidly now. The dialogue is taken to prove immortality of soul; we have seen that it is concerned with the philosophical soul, with Socrates' in particular, and with that soul as the principle of his human life, that is, with the immortality of philosophical discourse.

Socrates' response to Simmias is, in effect, that soul must be immortal or else evil would be impossible. To Cebes a hypothesis is set and, because immortality is one way of describing how the tenaciously clung to hypothesis works into daily life, immortality fits and is accepted. In each case the form of argument consists in positing the conclusion, and is thus invalid deductive argument. The only way it attains validity is if the argument is retrorsive, and this it can be only if it is concerned with itself. If there is no other way for there to be the evil of error which initiates dialogue, indeed which motivated the whole trial, and if the hypothesis clung to is not the absolutes but is the sole dogma, that life is better than death, then these arguments become retrorsive and valid.

By altering the usual focus of the dialogue through rhetorical and logical aids, it has become possible to validate what was invalid.[7]

WE HAVE ACTIVATED AND SO SUPPORTED THE CLAIMS, SOMEHOW: GRAMMAR (3)

If this is his point, can we receive it? How can we today sell our lives to proofs, as the rejection of misology requires? Surely Socrates is not asking for capitulation before the first clever sophist who comes to sell us. What he wants is a conditional acceptance of whatever point of view seems more solid at the stage we have reached, but of no point of view which makes any acceptance impossible; further, research after truth takes the direction of making clear whether a viewpoint does or does not support this, and how. This study has set the dialogue's words in their own proper context. At the same time, undertaking the study has joined in the effort, set it within a context created by our conjoined efforts, and thereby actively validated its claims. However, removing these claims from one perspective can validate them only if they are remythologized, and the ways in which this author has done so are not altogether clear to him.

NOTES

1. The texts are Tredennick's Bollingen English and Burnet's Oxford Greek.

2. H.S. Stern does not make clear that the absence is important, vexing instead the issue of why Plato would desert the deathbed and guessing that he was sick with grief, in "Plato's Funeral Oration", *The New Scholasticism* XLVIII (1974), 504.

3. Cp. Wagner, *Tristan und Isolde,* Act II, Scene 2: "Weiches Todes Streichen koennte je sie weichen? Stuend'er vor mir der maecht'ge Tod wie er mir Leib und Leben bedroht, die ich so wilig der Liebe lasse, Wie waere seinen Streichen die Liebe selbst zu erreichen? Stuerb'ich nun ihr der so gern ich sterbe, wie koennte die Liebe mit mir sterben, die ewig lebende mit mir enden? Doch stuerbe nie seine Liebe, wie stuerbe dann Tristan seiner Liebe?"

4. There is no need to belabor the problems with the arguments taken separately. Strabo, still speaking within the appropriate *phusis-logos* context, covers the argument heads quite adequately in his critique; see his appendix to Hackforth's *Plato's Phaedo*.

5. Cp. J.A. Stewart: "But if it cannot be explained moral responsibility may be pictured—pictured in a myth . . . not to be taken literally, but to be dwelt on ('it is necessary to sing this over to one's self'), till the charm of it touches one deeply"—so deeply that, when the 'uninitiated' say 'it is not true', one is able to answer by acting, as if it were true." *The Myths of Plato*, (London: Centaur Press, 1904), p. 133. Stewart stresses the substitute character of belief, whereas we stress its performative character.

6. Cp. E.G. Ballard: "The drift of the Platonic philosophy is in the main directed toward a grasp through myth and doctrine of communicable beliefs about the whole person within a universe where he is not an alien. A complete and definitive understanding of the person and his universe is prevented by the a-rational factor in both. Thus to pre-

serve his integrity he must continually bring his own nature into question." *Socratic Ignorance: An Essay on Platonic Self-Knowledge* (The Hague: Martinus Nijhoff, 1965), p. 182. Ballard's conclusion is the same, but ours is based not upon metaphysical composition but upon the mode of existing available to the unified human existent.

7. Cf. R. Guardini: "The 'proofs' do nothing more than interpret the awareness or experience that one's mind is more real the more he attends to the idea. ... The dialog is not a proof but a logos which interprets experience and brings the mind's life into action." *The Death of Socrates* (Sheed and Ward, 1948), pp. 112, 167. The difference between this mentalist bent and our carnal one should be evident.

CHAPTER TWO

PAIDEIA, SCHOLE, PAIDIA: THEN AND NOW

Paideia, the citizen's education, is extensively tied up with liberal studies in most of Aristotle's discussion in book eight of the *Politics*. But this tie-up intellectualizes the leisure at their root in the first few chapters of the book.

While my undergraduates in leisure studies always need to be drawn up from their sole focus upon sport, perhaps my philosophy colleagues need relief to de-intellectualize *paideia* back down to *schole*. There are dimensions of Aristotle's comments which are remedial to contemporary streams of leisure theory. This chapter will recapitulate his comments, then apply them to three types of contemporary theory.

His first chapter justifies the reason why politics is not meddling when it takes an interest in the formation of its citizens. This is because any constitution will not be workable unless citizens' characters, their virtues, are compatible with it.

His second chapter opens what should be taught. Without doubt, useful things should be taught. But not all useful things: useful things which "vulgarize" the citizen should not. To vulgarize is to make one less fit for the practice of virtue, the city's concern. Any occupation, art or science can vulgarize. An occupation will, if it is paid employment; that degrades the mind by absorbing it. An art will, if it deforms the body; the Spartans did that, by their excruciating and savage routines. And a science will, if it is pursued to its perfection of detail.

Our bywords about workaholic compulsions, steroid stars, and nerdy scholars, show that we experience the three instances he speaks of, even if paradoxes appear that do not trouble him. Why learn anything at all that is useful, if we can't earn a living at it? How is it virtuous to be never the master but ever a dabbler? Is it not inherent in science to drive us to its ultimate details, one way toward its principles and another toward its applications?

These three are more localized problems, however, than his fourth limitation on useful education. That the very same activity is first excluded from the teachable useful, and then is re-included merely by a change in its object, touches our Aristotle with an anachronistic subjectivity, whereby the subject constitutes whatever identity the object has. Excluded if done for others, a study is included if done for one's self, friends or virtue. Perhaps this can best be grasped as the learner's selection of the latter ends from among the complex of goals which attach objectively to a learnable study.

What follows comes naturally to our modern eye. "If he's excluded all employments, then of course all that left to talk about is leisure." To his eye, however, this is because leisure is the principle of all other activities [taking, with all translators, the αυτη of 1337b33 to refer to σχολωζειν, not the more plausible μουσικη or φυσις; as their reference at 1338a11 to σχολη, not the more likely ηδονη]. Leisure is central not as the residue from busyness but as its purpose and thus its meaning. Leisure is core to both the non-useful and the useful learning in *paideia*, even in the contracted "useful" which is properly taught.

Play is not excluded from leisure studies, as the four vulgarities are from useful studies; but care is taken not to equate them. Usually translated amusement, his *paidia* is closer to what we call recreation. That is, this activity is not the purpose of life, but instead contributes to something that is not our purpose. Work or toil is debilitating; no one would do it for its own sake. If anything, work is done for leisure. And, in turn, recreation is done in view of work, since it restores one from-and-for work. Unwinding is what gives pleasure; we all experience that.[1]

Leisure, on the other hand, involves pleasure with reference to nothing else. Pleasure comes from leisure's being already its end, in both modern senses: leisure has no goal but itself; and it drives forward to nothing else. It is a state, not a process, in our speech; it is practice not production, governed by prudence not art, in his speech. It is hard to keep from identifying it with happiness, instead of simply associating them as he does.

It is equally hard to keep from affirming that studies at leisure consist of music, in the comprehensive hellenic sense or the commonplace one Aristotle discusses through the end of the *Politics*. But this has not kept philosophers, psychologists and sociologists from coopting leisure to the practice of their own discipline as its heart, or at least its sole adequate statement.

Contemporary leisure theories range from completely objectifying leisure to completely subjectifying it, neither of which was among the errors available to a pre-Cartesian philosopher. At the objective end is the so-called "classical" theory of leisure, most famous in Pieper and DeGrazia,[2] and updated by Green.[3] To rest in whatever is eternal is the fullness of leisure. Short of God-given mysticism, leisure becomes speculative philosophy. Other activities share leisureliness to the degree they approximate philosophy.

Dispensing with gravitation around deity and the eternal, its more eleatic tack is made by Fink in the wake of Husserl, Heidegger, Gadamer, and by Rorty in Peirce's story. Leisure is the comprehensive category of life because it is the world which plays us, not vice-versa. The lifeworld of Fink and the conversation of Rorty are bounded, but by nothing, and so not necessitated by the whole, which the part can never appropriate and confirm.

What is noticeable is that Aristotle, for all his emphasis elsewhere upon undying reality and for all his invocation as the patron of the "classical" view, never ties up leisure to pure act, to the spheres which imitate it, or to our reproduction which strives for them. One hint of his unwillingness to philosophize leisure is his indecision whether the happy life is the speculative or the political, or whether happiness—so close to leisure in its pleasures, as has been seen—relates to the changeless or the changing. At the very least, whatever need he saw for eternity was satisfied in his *Ethics* by the autotelism of doing rather than of making, with no need to invoke the virtue of scientific necessity in order to purchase enough footing for leisure.

The temporal category dear to the classical theory is "diurnal" time. This is the time of large and recurring natural units, to avoid frantic disintegration of actions into the separate fragments which things have, especially machines, more especially clocks. Its eternity drives Pieper and DeGrazia; the unavailability of this value to us today drives Green to jettison classical leisure from the paideia he'd have liked to set up.

Even without it, the following is available. The merit of Huizinga's work,[4] contemporary to Pieper's and unmarginalized by its apt criticisms in Callois' and Ehrmann's developments, is to locate in play the features which provide sufficient local eternity to satisfy the needs of classical leisure theory. Playtime is distinguished from other times. It is set apart, and its temporal units have meaning only from the inside; the sets of tennis, the innings of baseball, have nothing to do with the passage of minutes and seconds. Even the timed periods of other major sports are bent by timeouts, incompletions, delays, penalties defined in their rules and nowhere else. The rules themselves, the costuming, the venues, the identifying of players and non-players hive off a world that is self-contained. Its experience is not so much the one of derivative pleasure for which Aristotle rejected paidia or play, as it is the completeness of the event. Classical leisure can be as fully realized in these pedestrian and democratic forms of sports, of games, and of narratives, as in the exacting and excluding forms of speculative philosophy.

A second contemporary theory of leisure takes and turns this objective formation into its opposite. Csikszentmihalyi and colleagues[5] affect the social psychologists' factual objectivity while driven by the critical theorists' moral imperatives. Less the self-containment of Huizinga's play than its rule-boundedness, is what these theorists take up. They locate experiences similar to reports of "discovering something new", "exploring a strange place", or "solving a problem". These activities have no external payoffs, but people pursue them anyway. The activities are "autotelic", they contain their own goals. Thus far their objectivity.

In parsing out what makes these activities autotelic, he finds that there is a definite sense of control within them. The activities are ones whose challenges are suited to the participant's capabilities, whose procedures are not ambiguous but are spelled out in rules, and whose feedback is clear and quick enough for the participant to know how well he or she has succeeded. These make up "flow" experiences. Joining in these activities brings satisfaction, which he distinguishes from pleasure; pleasure is attached to fulfilling basic needs, to consumption, to consumer substitutes for autotelic activities.

Each person has one's own level of capability; and so the opportunities which each decides to challenge those skills against, and the rules upon which feedback will occur, differ for each. That is to say, it is not the activities which are autotelic, but the agents. They seek each his or her own idiosyncratic end. No comprehensive norms stand by to check the uprightness of this leisure. Only its being autotelic is its norm; and that is different for each.

Csicszentmihalyi tries to save his doctrine from this psychological subjectivity by stressing that social construction of reality is always at work. But this sits as mere moralizing atop what is fundamentally a scientific solipsism. Small matter that, verbally, Csiczentmihalyi opposes flow experience to leisure; this is only because of his taking leisure in the sense of consumer activity, freetime from work, time free to use up for one's own pleasures.

Has Aristotle anything to help out with, here? First, it is clear that what is autotelic for him is the activity, not the agent. Leisure is what is an end in itself; the agent does not seek differently than leisure or the state of happiness for his end.

Next, pleasure is not simply set apart from the satisfaction of leisure; pleasure accompanies it, although pleasure is not its goal (if ever it can be a goal). The pleasure is a sign that taking leisure is as natural as consuming for the political animal. For leisure he need construct no abstruse postkantian satisfaction uncorrupted by pleasure.

Finally, "the pleasure of the best person is the best, and comes from the best sources" (1138a9). Does this reduce the subjectivity of satisfactions, or reinforce it? The best person is the most virtuous; virtues are attuned by mediating the circumstances each person meets, "the right thing at the right time . . ."; the circumstances each meets and their meaning which each mediates are peculiar to each one's culture and society; so being the best man is relative to these local meanings. Does this only replace individual relativity with social relativity? That will be discussed next; but, here, the point is that it appears do at least that.

A third contemporary reference point upon leisure philosophy is the communitarian. While not as visibly represented in leisure monographs (see Mason[6]), it coordinates leisure studies to the eighties' political philosophy of communitarianism, and its cultural precipitate in political correctness. Correspondences could be perceived, if one wished, between intellectualist or metaphysical leisure, and the resurgent liberalism of the forties; between freetime leisure, and the scientistic economism in service to the industrial ethos of the fifties; between "flow" leisure, and the sixties' and seventies' refusal of consumerism by the negativities in critical theory. In the libertarian nineties, thinking about leisure-through-downsizing was made invisible by such devices as Canada's renaming unemployment insurance as "employment insurance".

The communitarian insight is that people's relationships form their identity equally as much as do their individualities. At an extreme, relation completely forms their reality. The liberal error was to think that relata precede relations; the communitarian correction is to say that relations precede relata. While the former makes it impossible to ascribe significance to relations, communitarian thought makes it difficult to describe how any new relations could ever be formed, much less how a person could form them by him or herself.

The application of communitarian philosophy to leisure emerges in the insistence that any leisurely activity be in the service of community. Therapeutic recreation, adaptive sports, remedial reading, interventionist travel, music-studio-drama therapy: these become the sole upright manners to perform leisure; for "when one is [deprived], all are [deprived]", using the form but not the content of rights theory. Leisure is set toward an extrinsic end, the betterment of others; but in the communitarian framework, this is not external since the others are identified with me.

The moral claustrophobia this imposes upon the ελευθερος who is Aristotle's man-at-leisure can be remedied by returning to the "best man" once again, to finish the description of his or her pleasures. It is not only in view of the virtues peculiar to one's own society that someone's pleasures are best; for that society itself may be judged as more or as less a reservoir of virtue. Aristotle, in fact, never ceases judging his and others' societies severely; nor is his judgment nothing but ethnocentric (although it is surely that, too). For the virtues he demands are not those which perfect being hellene, but which perfect being humane. In his eye, hellenic society (often) succeeds best at that; but other societies are contemptible not because they are not humane, but because they fail humans. Their societies have degraded, "vulgarized", some feature or another of what it is to be human—body, or mind; courage, or articulateness, etc.

The paragon of leisure is connected; but he or she is also autotelic. This person is articulate, but in play as well as in science, craft, work and politics. This paragon, therefore, is not beyond the reach of any person. While the details of the paideia towards it remain to be fleshed out, as they did for Aristotle, nonetheless preserving these insights from one revealer of our humanness should block a few of the blind alleys in designing the paideia for leisure.

NOTES

1. Bernard Suits, *The Grasshopper: Games, Life and Utopia*. (U. Toronto, 1978).
2. Josef Pieper, *Leisure; The Basis of Culture*. (New York NY: Random House, 1970).

3. Thomas F. Green, *Work, Leisure and the American Schools*. (New York NY: Random House, 1970).

4. Johann Huizinga *Home Ludens; A Study of the Play Element in Culture*. (Boston: Beacon, 1950).

5. Mikail Csikszentmihalyi,. *Beyond Boredom and Anxiety; The Experience of Play in Work and Games*. (San Francisco CA: Jossey Bass, 1975),.and with Robert Kubey. *Television and the Quality of Life; How Viewing Shapes Everyday Experience*.(Lawrence KS: Erlbaum, 1990).

6. Sheila Mason, and Randy B. Swedburg. "Education for Leisure: Moving Toward Community." (Denver CO: 2d Int. Symp. on Leisure & Ethics, 11 Apr. 1994).

CHAPTER THREE

FINALITY'S FLAMEOUT

Aristotle's startling comparison of the human knower and the divine knower never fails to provide stimulus for reflective projects. It may be the locus for solving how divine being is the sole substance causally explanatory of other substances; and, in turn, how divine science or first philosophy of being qua being can be the supervisory science over the philosophies of the various genera of substances of which being is said in its many ways.

Most engaging and crucial is the way in which divine substance may be said to know. To explicate thought thinking thought, it can be said that what the divine thinks is the forms of separated substance which, in being thought actually, are one with the actuality of divine thinking.

This already takes account of the difference between the human knower and the divine, but doesn't take full account of it. The human's knowing faculty has no identity until it knows objects other than itself because, as capable of all, it cannot be any but is in unbounded potency. The divine thinker is also said to have no identity of its own except for its objects. The reason for saying this of the human, however, is absent from the divine. Divine intellect is never in potency for all that it can know, but is always knowing its objects actually.

How does this difference reflect upon the self-identity which the divine knower knows? Rather than nothing in being before it knows, it is always actually in being. Its identity is not achieved or even just made available by its knowing of other objects. It has its identity with knowing, without that following upon any time or state when it was not knowing.

Does this mean, however, that knowing activity (cartesian or otherwise) can be the first known for the divine knower, even though it cannot be the first known for the human knower? Or at least known no later than its knowledge of its objects? That would be the case only if the activity of knowing intellectually were different from its object. It is not different by priority in time. It is not different by priority in essence, since it is postulated to be identical. But if it is no different at all from its objects, then divine knowing folds back into its objects, and it becomes unnecessary to postulate one of those two, divine being or else its objects, at all.

The very least that can be said is that, for the divine, there is no intramental activation to prepare for intellectual knowing, no contextualizing of it during the knowing, and no interpretation, no inferences thereafter. There is none of the "psychological" baggage with which the human knower can be identified prior to her knowing intellectually; succinctly, again, there is no potentiality for knowing. There is simply the identity of knower and known that knowledge chases as its perfection. The divine knowing is fullest achievement of "the knower in act is the known in act", for the knower is never not in act.

But is the known ever not in act? Is it ever something other than its actuality of being known divinely? Even if that knowing is never in potency to know its objects, they are at some time in potency to be known by divine knowing,. The rest of the algorithm for knowledge then comes into play: the knower becomes the known, but not in the way the known exists. This is clearest when the known exists materially; the knower become his object, without assuming the object's materiality. But it is also the case when the known is immaterial, a separated form; the knower becomes that object, without being assimilated to its singularity. Knowing one separated substance that is the intelligence of one celestial movement, is not knowing another and different celestial intelligence. A human knower may know one, and be ignorant of another. The divine knower cannot. But a human knower may know both, and know that one is not the other. And this the divine knower must do as well. It must be one in knowing with each of them; but its kinship with one of them is not its kinship with the other of them, however coherent and systematic are its several knowings. And if they are different in the knowing, all the more are they different in their being.

The difference is part of what divine knowing comprehends, as well. In addition, because it comprehends their differences from each other, it comprehends its difference from them. It could not be the unity it is, without being different from the differences they bear. Being different from them, it is something itself; and this not by an indeterminate potentiality such as characterizes the human knower before her knowing, but by a never unactualized difference and self-identity. We do not penetrate what that is, of course; but, whatever it is, it remains there as what the divine knower could know of itself, different from the forms of the other objects it knows.

Thus there need not be a restriction of its objects of knowing to the separated forms which need no abstraction from matter in order for them to be known. The divine knower could know even the forms that are complementary to matter, without having to abstract them of course, for this does not diminish the divine knowing, which is already distinct in identity and so needing assimilation even to its more perfect objects other than itself, namely the separated intelligences.

Aristotle already said that this merger of thought with everything that is because of their kinship is mistaken (429b30). It is only potentially that thought and its objects have kinship and, prior to that, its objects are simply what they are. While the thinking mind actually is those distinct formal objects that it thinks, and so forms are not inferior to it, but are identical to it as the objective counterpart of its self-thinking, this means that the divine mind is identified with them; it does not mean that they are identified with the divine mind. Although mind and thing are identified in neither direction for the human knower, except in the very act of intellectual cognition, at least one of those non-identities remains in the divine knowing; and that is enough to keep it from being immanent to all natural knowings.

For divine knowing does not grasp forms as an indivisible whole. However much divine knowing holds together relations of genus, species and differentiae in a single and eternal act of cognition; however systematic that cognition may be, the divine cognition will still be erroneous if it thinks its objects lack differences between genuses, and especially among things, *tode tis*.

Working backwards, however, have we lost anything that we needed by denial of this claim, tempting as it was? It seems so, if my suggestion makes divine thinking referential to itself in a way that makes knowledge of the subordinate substances impossible. That would be the case if its self-knowing is the *immanent* telos of all natural functions, That might seem to be the case because, otherwise, divine substance could provide no more than an external telos of substances, and so not provide an adequate reference for the *pros hen* universality that establishes the dominance of their sciences under first philosophy.

Is that the case, however? Such a cognitional if not idealist strategy would replace some medievals' strategy of looking to divine efficient causation from the *Physics* to explain the genera ("perfections") of things. But he and they agree that final causation is not enough to explain them. Or at least external final causation would not be enough. Immanent final causation would. That strategy would replace immanent final cause with immanent formal.

But why is their striving to imitate divine self-return in the suggestive *De Anima* passage not sufficient for what is needed? The process of final causation is one in which the first heaven seeks self-thinking by its circular motion, the celestial bodies seek the circular by their elliptical, and natural bodies seek the elliptical by their processes of generation and corruption. That process is external, so it seems not to penetrate the essential nature of sensible substance, nor to be determining it immanently, because that process is physical and indirect. As such, an external final cause cannot give essential determination to various substances; only an immanent formal cause can do that.

The insufficiency of divine final causation seems to lie in its being physical and indirect. That is, the movements caused by final causation in natural bodies are an unforeseen and accidental consequence of motion inspired in the first heaven. But being unforeseen and accidental is never an obstacle to the efficacy of final causation except in human deliberative conduct, a narrow range since neither sub- nor super-human reality engages in deliberation.

Nor is the reference to the physical elements of heat and cold a problem, for again there is no foreignness of final causation to physical processes, even elemental ones.

The complaint may be that final cause cannot namely provide the essential determinations of sensible substances. The formal principle does that, and for supra-sensible substances as well. Surely the problem here is not that only formal and material are called internal by Aristotle, while final and efficient are called external. For that categorial distance is handily surpassed by the assimilation he makes between formal and final causation, even closer than the approximation he allows between formal and efficient.

If the problem is that the single divine finality should issue in a single formality celestial and sublunary, an obliteration of the variety among genera, perhaps the response can be that the reception of form in matter—a principle immune to explanation by divine finality—provides explanation not only of numerical multiplicity but also of qualitative variety. Substance embodies its yearning for divine self-return to whatever extent, i.e. in whatever form, the receiving matter makes possible.

In view of that, divine finality direct or intermediate may be enough to provide the unity of the essential being of various substances, which the identity of divine knowing with its objects seems not to provide. If so, the subordination of sciences to theology while maintaining their own autonomy may be equally feasible. The universality not of a genus but of a reference by analogy fits the repeated example the Philosopher uses—that of the reference to health by food, by physician, by exercise-and fits the example better when it is reference of all these means to health as their finality, rather than as their formality. Even the verbal syntax of *pros hen* is better fitted to finality.

If so, then the ordering and autonomy of sciences may be less problematic than appears. Their ordering occurs, because what is assumed as first principle and is not proven in the lower science, is proven as a theorem in the higher science. Their autonomy is assured, because the theorems of the lower are not proven in the higher, nor in any of the other sciences taking a different theorem of the same higher as their first principle.

In terms of the final process above, the autonomy of the sciences concerning sublunary genera of substances does not dispense with the sciences of celestial substance, in order to dash madly into a conflagration with the science of the divine final cause. Each performs, in order, its own task and identifies its own finalities.

All except human science, whose shocking presence of seemingly divine knowing right within it provokes us to jettison its order, yield its autonomy, and rush home immediately. I'm suggesting we resist the provocation.

CHAPTER FOUR

EXTERNAL GOODS AND CONTEMPLATION IN ARISTOTLE

From reading the first and last books of the *Nicomachean Ethics* one might think that, in Aristotle's view, the politician shares with the philosopher in the activity of contemplation, which makes the life of each to be fully happy.[1] One way Aristotle treats that there is by comparing the necessity of external goods for the politican and for the philosopher. The provoking issue to be treated at the end of this chapter is the possible content of this shared life of contemplation, after studying the claim itself.

Initially no one would be surprised that politics is prominent in this ethics, even where it is the philosopher who is addressed; for it is a commonplace confirmed by its first and last books that ethics is but the preface to the politics which follow.

Nor would one be surprised that the activity of contemplation depends upon the political life. For the essence of the city gets defined in terms of a completeness not equivalent to achieving better the necessities of wealth and security or even of friendship, but a completeness equivalent to communicating in speech together about the good life; the city in speech opens the only space where good life involving contemplation is made possible at all and then preserved.

Another reason not to be surprised that contemplation depends upon politics, is that contemplative activity exercises the faculty of a soul which depends upon souls characterized by prior faculties; but the latter do not depend upon it (*De Anima* 2, 2). Contemplation provides a unique approach to truth which depends upon more basic ones, while they do not depend on it (*Meta.* 1, 1). This non-symmetrical "nesting" of contemplation among the series of faculties keeps it from ever being hived off from their politics, into the goal for any ascetic ethical pursuit.

The political life does involve a significant amount of external goods and the moral virtues for using them, while philosophical life involves somewhat less of both. But in neither life are external goods either unnecessary, nor are they intrinsically necessary. Instead the goods are more or less necessary only as conditions for the moral virtues; these are essential to the respective lives, and those in turn as lives of happiness.

This conjunction may let it appear that philosophical life or the life of contemplation requires more goods than only the activity of contemplation; and that political life or the life of practical virtue involves the activity of contemplation and not only the external goods with which action according to practical virtue is concerned.

A distinction between the lives of happiness and the activities of happiness is an increasingly common solution.[2] However plausible that may be, two further distinctions tend to meld, as well, but need some further discernment. One is among the terms political, practical, external and fortune, often used for one another. The other distinction is within the set of terms loosely bound to necessary conditions or intrinsic ones.

External goods are not essential parts of a life of happiness, nor are they only instrumentally necessary conditions by addition. External goods are necessary as goods *intrinsically* necessary in addition to the essential parts of each life of happiness; it would be a mistake to find no distinction in Aristotle between goods necessary instrumentally, and those necessary intrinsically although only by addition. The only possible claim, then, is that external goods are necessary and intrinsic though not essential to each form of life; it would be senseless to say that essential goods were essential to the philosophical life, and uninteresting to say only that they could add something to it. This also makes it maintainable that two forms of life differ not qualitatively by their need for external goods, but only qualitatively or as a matter of degree.

The other set of distinctions come closer to the heart of the matter. Goods called external are not the same as goods by fortune; for intrinsic goods as well, such as character traits, may also suffer loss by misfortune, or acquisition by mere moral luck. The term 'practical' applies to virtues, not goods; but practical (or moral) virtue concerns the use of external goods. Lastly, political life and virtue concern not merely external goods but also the intrinsic, and involve practical virtues collectively but not individually. The ambiguity of "goods" throughout many languages infects this topic, too; it is used not of things in themselves, like drygoods, nor of things only so far they reflect our evaluations of them as good for us; 'goods' names the former assumed to be the latter, but without testing that assumption.

These clarifications make it easier to understand the claim that external goods are necessary conditions to any life of happiness, whether political or philosophical, intrinsically, although only by addition or instrumentally.

Upon this sorting of goods, the discussion of contemplation can be imposed. Political life is also happy to the fullest extent, not only because Aristotle says so in the first book but also because he allows so in book ten. Book ten allows this, because the political life is not devoted only to practical virtues, for these aim beyond themselves. It may seem obvious that what they aim at is contemplation, and that this is the only reasonable alternative.

Some difficulties with these conclusions arise, however. Simply because politics aims at and promotes contemplation, is no reason to say that the politican has access to contemplation; sharing with the philosopher a need for external goods is not a reason to say that. Nor is the fact that his life culminates in contemplation a reason to say that the politican indulges in contemplation. Even that there is some sort of natural culmination of politics' practical virtue of prudence, in philosophy's intellectual virtue of contemplation, does not show the politician's contemplation without further ado; for the manifold of persons with full panoply of moral virtue, but without a stitch of contemplative bent, requires that the "nesting" of faculties mentioned previously be made much more muscular, before we could infer that people can't help being contemplative once they're virtuous. Would that were so; then our multidisciplinary students could parley their lived successes and their skills in other subjects into instant success in philosophy!

This consideration has impact also on the primary reasons for this claim. First, it is true that the politician is the architect of happiness of the state, of the life which includes the activity of contemplation. But she need not live in the house she builds, in order for her to build it for the philosopher. Plato's conclusion in the *Meno*, that actions go just as well when run by opinion as when guided by knowledge, does more than enough to undo his *Republic*'s persuasions, that only a philosopher-king can deliver justice. Aristotle's statement in starting his *Metaphysics*, that people don't seek the wisdom found in universals, by craft or contemplation, in order to get their jobs done any better, goes more than far enough to undo any suggestion that doing politics brings contemplation in its wake. Even though both craft and contemplation are within the range of wisdom, one never equates the other; craft does not have to depend upon contemplation before it can occur, does not have to issue in contemplation after it occurs. Would that were so; then our philosophy majors could reassure their long-suffering parents that eventually they'll make a difference, and a buck!

No more does identifying the politican as contemplator or philosopher follow from realizing that there can be persons of practical virtue who are not political rulers. For these persons may well not be political rulers, without being philosophers and contemplators, either; they are more likely the persons who live practical virtue outside of political office. Of course in Pericles' Athens if not in Aristotle's they are always "political" in the wider sense of being self-making along with others; but that is not at issue. So much the more is this so when the political life contrasted with this private life is the despotic political life.

The contrast of the private person with the politician seems to be another reason to share contemplation among the persons of practical virtue, public or private, along with the philosopher; it is not the politician who is the object of contrast with the philosopher in this contrast of practical and speculative. But that does nothing to show that contemplation will be found there in fact, and less that it is a life of happiness which shares this same activity of intellectual virtue.

One suggestion that reconciles these claims is to attend not to lives nor to virtues, but to the primary substances or persons who activate them both. The same person can have a political life and a philosophical life, can be happy in each by activating practical virtue both moral and intellectual in one, and activating the speculative intellectual virtue of contemplation in the other. The lives are neither confused, nor opposed; the happinesses are not separate, but distinct. The need for external goods differs only by being more pronounced in the former. Aristotle did not say that; his principles surely permit him to. His civilization probably did not.

Notice that as presented there is complete symmetry within happiness between the kind of life, the kind of virtue, and its kind of good. Happiness in political life is concerned with moral virtue regarding external goods of fortune, practical virtue; and happiness in philosophical life is concerned with speculative intellectual virtues regarding the internal good of contemplation. But of significant absence is where the *practical intellectual* virtues fit into this symmetry.

The practical intellectual virtue of prudence or *phronesis* is concerned with the very stuff of politics; its activity of doing or *praxis* is the self-making of human identity in public that completes the person's own self-making. In both of these the doing is equivalent to ethics or the search for happiness. The practical intellectual virtue of craft or *techne* does not apply to politics, for its activity of making or *poiesis* is not done upon community. Making is only done upon those outcomes which are separable from the maker and have a termination of their own apart from hers.

In contrast, doing has the same feature that contemplation or *theoria* has, namely, it concerns what is inherently unending. While contemplation's objects have been and will be forever the way they are, eternal, the objects of doing are natural objects which have a beginning and an end, namely, ourselves and our societies. But as mortal reproduction emulates self-thinking life, so does this political cognate of contemplation cherish and protect the fully speculative mode of contemplation.

This is why leisure as the deeper stratum of happiness does not have to be confined to the well-to-do. Aristotle treats leisure first as an amateur anthropologist of wealth, finding leisure only to occur in societies like Egypt where slave-driven civilization and wealth first had reached an advanced level. But he also supplies its metaphysical side, that leisure occurs whenever people can focus on what is undying, even if eternal only for as long as the narrow confines of their own nature and cities last, or for us in books and parties and games. Not only a Senate seat, but any WWF match brings one close to the life of contemplation; so does the appreciation of self-thinking thought. Perhaps this approaches as far as Aristotle allows to contemplation in the political life.

NOTES

1. Especially at 1099a32–b8, 1099b25–34 and 1178b33–9a9. A sample of this reading might be gleaned from R. Heinmann, "Eudaimonia and Self-Sufficiency in the Nicomachean Ethics," *Phronesis* 33 (1988), 31. Variants occur, up through A. Kenny, "The Nicomachean Conception of Happiness," in H. Blumenthal and H. Robinson, eds. *Oxford Studies in Ancient Philosophy* (supplementary volume) (Oxford: Clarendon Press, 1991), 67. Roopen Majithia directed me these texts.

2. See n. 1.

CHAPTER FIVE

ARISTOTLE'S TEXT ON JUSTICE

> Της δε κατα μερος δικαιοσυνης και του κατ'αυτην δικαιον εν μεν εστιν ειδος το εν ταις *διανομαις*... εν δε το εν ταις *συναλλαγμαις* διορθωτικον.
>
> The form of partial justice, and of what is just by it, that occurs in *distributions* . . . is distinguished from the other form of it that occurs in *transactions*.
>
> N.E., V, 2, 1130b30–1131a1[1]

This text of Aristotle's is as disputed as it is famous. One particular version of it is of importance for contemporary legal philosophy, the version of Ernest Weinrib,[2] professor of law and of classics at the University of Toronto. This chapter will suggest that Weinrib's version can be increased in power by reappropriating the text in a different version, one fortified by the commentary and thought of Thomas Aquinas.[3]

The substantive claim in this study is that Weinrib can rely upon the text not only for his distinction between the forms of justice, but also for the normativity in the justices so distinguished. The distinction is important, because Weinrib's reliance upon it is catalytic in his reorientation of modern private law onto one of these forms, and to a lesser extent public law upon the other. Its normativity is equally important to restore, because Weinrib feels compelled to turn from Aristotle to Kant for that, with results less attractive than they might have been.

The procedural claim in this study, however, is more to the theme of textuality. This is the claim that recognition of the contexts for texts is indispensible for their correct understanding and use. Aristotle's text and these segments of its history serve as an example for the deployment of this interpretative method.

The method consists in supplying various sorts of contexts for texts. Any text stands as an artifact among others of the same sort, words among which it is located, not only the words written or said, but those which remain unsaid from which the said were selected: its grammar. Any text also stands as a sign over against existents of a different sort, namely, the things which are its referents, the understandings which are its meanings, including again those which remain present though unmentioned: its logic. And any text stands before a set of auditors or readers, whose comprehension is anticipated and informs the text, as well as those who are excluded from it by intent or by circumstance: its rhetoric.

These "trivia" supply the most prominent contexts, if not all. Each is unbounded,and requires a limitation of scope; all events are the text's context, but interpretion is only a human enterprise. Even the distinction between the trivial contexts involves selection since, for example, the text may be about other words (its logic), and not simply among them (its grammar). The selection of contexts relies in part upon the very history it is meant to clarify; so the fact that Weinrib looks to Aquinas (as well as to Hegel, Stammler, and thereby Kant) to confirm his own claims about Aristotle is one factor in choosing Aquinas as a reference point in this treatment of the text, instead of the numerous Greek platonists, Islamic scholars, Medieval latinists, and European moderns who have commented upon Aristotle's text, in the sixteen hundred years from Aristotle to Aquinas, and the seven hundred from then to now.

DIANOMÉ AND *SYNALLAGMA* IN ARISTOTLE

Grammar

The placement of this text is in a chapter dealing with one kind of justice, the partial justice which is evidenced by the practices of praising, and blaming for failing to deal equally. This stands in contrast to a preceding chapter on the complete justice which is largely a matter of praise and blame for lawabiding. The following three chapters provide metaphors for the legal and the partial, as well as for the latter's two sorts, then locate their relevance to the economic and political orders, and lastly discuss their voluntariness. The book ends with phenomena which escape these formulations, the uniqueness of equity.

The last chapter of the book, querying justice towards oneself, returns these reflections on justice to the thrust of the preceding two books. For they are concerned with fortitude and temperance which, just as prudence in the following book, relate to an individual's own self. Justice is special in that, unlike these, it occurs only between several persons. What is not to be overlooked, however, is that it is not an equality between these several persons which serves as the equality with which justice is concerned. Instead, justice is concerned with the equality between each person's desert and his or her holdings. Justice consists in the habit of rendering up this equality.

Even though justice is found in this intermediate location, and thus promises its political relevance, its direction by an intellectual trait, prudence, is problematic since inhumanity escapes it—vicious, weak or corrupted by pleasure in books six and seven, or removed by the life of contemplation in the last. The remedy is friendship because it is both a care for the virtue of (some) other persons, and is simultaneously a shaggy template for political relationships. Aristotle can proceed from ethics to politics.

But facilitating politics by care for virtue returns his research to its opening concerns, that ethics is a matter of ends, that our end is happiness, and that happiness is parsed out as virtues, in books one and two. It is because human capacities are ours to fulfill, and their fulfilments constitute our state of happiness, that doing justice as one of those virtues is a morally good practice, an obligatory one. Justice is unique in that the just person attends not to himself but to providing the right holdings for persons, perhaps even by looking in prudence at the right relation among the other, individualistic virtues in order to bring this about. But, unique in this way, it has in common with the others that they involve moral goodness by nothing other than their being perfections of human capabilities, the very notion of happiness.

Nothing is said in these chapters of how these kinds of justices are forms, *eidoi*. But enough is said elsewhere; the volume wherein this text of Aristotle is found, is itself situated among the works of Aristotle. These works are not shy at explaining how each substance is capable of change, change which exercises to the full the limited share in being which each has. Among these capacities for change within its kind are species-distinctive capacities to act in order to initiate change, including change in those same capacities, for their betterment or worsening, initiated by oneself.

These are words which are not said, to amplify the *eidoi* in the chapter under discussion; but those unsaid words make possible those which are said. When they become said, later in history, only then to be denied, this denial makes it impossible to continue saying what Aristotle did not find it necessary to say here: that justice and its kinds is a sufficiently compelling moral obligation for it to underpin the law into which politics issues.

Logic

As the use of *eidos* in this passage indicates, the reference points Aristotle struggles with are platonic remainders. They always threaten to overwhelm his discourse as referents, and not only as meanings. What Aristotle is struggling to repossess is the equivalent to form, *morphé,* but on the human and cultural plane, where the counterpart to the matter, *hylé,* has become less plausible. He is seeking what is natural, the nature of the ethical human and of her social interactions, where that human engages in acting upon her own nature to perfect it or to flaw it by virtue or vice.

This is not a nature created for the person, nor is it one she creates for herself. Those are not denied, they are not even said so that they can be denied.

They remain unsaid as possibilities of the text which it remains for Aquinas and for Weinrib, respectively, among others to open.

Rhetoric

The text of Aristotle is placed before students who have a contemporary experience of the Academy in its skeptical phase, but not as strong as Aristotle's recall of its Master at his best, committed to politics by his metaphysics. Imperial subjects, they have that much less the memory of the Periclean *polis* which modelled his commitments. Aristotle's address to them cannot evoke the justice of equality among citizens by reason of their sharing in ruling and being ruled, but only the equality of each in view of his private stake. Equality of persons is not denied, it is simply out of sight, for now. Friendship can only approximate it.

DISTRIBUTIO AND *COMMUTATIO* IN AQUINAS

Grammar

The text in which Aquinas treats of Aristotle's distinction between the forms of justice is terse, and makes explicit few of Aristotle's unspoken dimensions. What it does do is to install a discourse which, with much greater frequency than the neuter *dikaion* in Aristotle, makes the term *justum* into the reference point of justice. This or *id quod est justum* presents justice with an objectivity so apparent that it remains tacit.

The just is not justice as an abstraction, nor the just person as its concrete agent. The term for the just thing points to a space of rightness from which the terms for virtue and agent are derivative in usage. The space is filled by characterizations of the deeds which bring the just thing into that space.

Virtue being now happiness as a continuing endstate does not cancel, but intensifies, virtue as the person's success in reaching the lifestate proper to his kind. This becomes somewhat less unspoken when Aquinas takes his own voice later in the "treatise on justice" within his summas, than it is within his commentary on Aristotle's vision of justice.[4] But in neither text has the issue become problematic, such that the practice called justice is firmly in place and is clearly described, but its normativity is lacking to it and needs be sought elsewhere.

The words of Aristotle on which Aquinas comments are new to his milieu. Coming to grips with them is what his words are set upon. The words which his must join are neither those familiar in the Lombard, nor the fresh ones which his summary manuals will later employ. By the same token, neither are they scripturally bound, for reaching Aristotle's words with his own may be quite heterodox, and still be accurate. But it is unlikely that the words of a faith comprehending all truth will not be found presaged there in his text.

Logic

The institutional reference point for the discourses on justice are the concrete deeds which instantiate the *obligatio* of Roman law. Found neither in one party to an agreement nor in the other, it too occupies the legal space between them, such that if one fails the commitment, the other is not free to breach his side of it thereafter.

A novel stature for the referents of discourse is what allows the just to be situated like this. The world of things is no longer made up of referents which simply bear their meanings as a matter of fact. While within nature, and existing in whatever way they do, they are now created nature, allowing response to a subjectivity whose intent places them into being. It is not the parameters of human justice which are set into being as it is. What is set into being is: that being is, the human being, the balance of whose capacities this virtue improves. That being may have to draw out those lines herself for justice; but they are the outer boundaries of her virtual reality, and no more mere swathes across empty space than they are simple tracings over fact. The giving of meaning by creation, however, does not displace the meaning that can be found in nature. Theorists of justice can always fall back upon the insights of Aristotle; but they will never be quite the same, since the advent of subjectivity upon those objective meanings will stay, elsewhere if not in creative deity and the human response to it.

Rhetoric

Aquinas' interlocutors for his comments on Aristotle are the Arts students and faculty, preparing for theology or for the Roman law reargued in Lombardy. Newly released from reliance upon platonizing texts of Aristotle by his recent translations, they need no longer be warned off of mistaking the objectivity of "the just thing" for something in its own right, rather than for the form of a relationship among people.

For this is the locale which the civil law obligation held: the relation no longer between only the thing and its claimant, but among claimants to that thing. Whether lay or clerical citizens of newly free cities, or even more free from local ordinaries as members of new Orders answering only to Rome, Aquinas' audience see again a role for themselves in shaping public life, rather than having to accept the place available for them in feudal dependency. Their role in forming justice has become conceptually possible again, coordinate with the justice in human nature formed by God.

DISTRIBUTION AND *TRANSACTION* IN WEINRIB

Grammar

The text which Aristotle wrote draws a distinction which, for Ernest Weinrib, is canonical. It gives the "form" of law, or better the forms of law since few words of his relate to what law is as a whole. But law is of justice; and justice is of two sorts, not one.

Weinrib's words to this effect occur in his chapter on "Corrective Justice", and make the same claim that a quarter century of his writing in law journals had done. They penetrate and accurately explain the meaning of Aristotle in his expression of the two forms of justice.

Where he adds words beyond Aristotle's is in his explanation of justice as an equality. The equality is between legal persons; and, in corrective justice, it is lost when a contract is breached (Aristotle's "voluntary" transaction) or when a tort is committed ("involuntary" transaction). It is also lost in distributions, which distributive justice is called to correct; but few words are spent on that.

While Aristotle's words in the two chapters following his focal text, where he develops mathematical metaphors for the two, can suggest equality of persons, that suggestion occurs only to a modern reader. The location of equality in his own words is as stated before: between prestations, or between proportions.

What prompts Weinrib's claim is the remainder of his text, here and earlier, which is a rejection of the writings by other prominent jurists (Epstein, Posner, Fried, Fletcher, Unger, Coleman) to the effect that distributions should be made within transactions (e.g., finding liability because of ability to pay, from deep commercial pockets or from healthy insurance coverage; or because of the need to punish, despite the absence of fault or wrongdoing within the transaction). He does not fail to write about many disadvantages of their claim in practice, but he devotes most words to its cognitive opaqueness. The opaqueness needs no argument, since admitted by the claim's proponents; but the alternative clarity of these two forms' excluding each other is what the words are addressed to.

The word "form" is used to describe these two kinds of law. But Aristotle's sense is no longer put into words; i.e., no longer is the counterpart to matter, but only to content (*Materie* and *Inhalt*, in dialectical philosophy) mentioned. The reason for this he says is destruction of confidence about form in nature, due to loss of faith in the knowledge of it. Forms as "chimeras" of men's minds is cited with approval from Locke (97 *Yale L.J.* 949 at 961); but this reference evokes the scorn for "species" in the individual's knowing from Bacon onward, which is only enhanced by critique based in social construction of reality for the past two centuries.

What sort of normativity can attach to such form? None but what the agent puts there; but none which resides in the developmental dynamic of the human person. And such an idiosyncratic injection gets no purchase upon anyone else's conduct.

If not the human being, however, then the rational being supercedes this. For reason cannot operate without the acknowledgement of all other rational beings as also self-constructing, the very notion of freedom and dignity which Kant derived from Rousseau's self-determination. In the human construct of private law, particularly, the equality of agents is most affirmed because their self-determination of entitlements is most voluntary and throughgoing. This is the text of the chapter on "Kantian Right" with which Weinrib follows that on corrective justice.

Weinrib's words thus have slid normativity, even the need for any search for normativity, into the space left silent in Aristotle's text, a space which never needed to be filled. Only change in the discourse on nature—another, much larger, but much more told tale—creates the space in Aristotle's words which requires Weinrib's in the discourse on justices. Once opened, however, it may now be filled in ways not only conflictual with Aristotle on nature, but also consistent with it.

Logic

The legal practice Weinrib speaks of is not one utterly at odds with his recommendations. For that practice is structured by the distinctions in Western law between public and private, distribution and transaction, embedded in the notion of the rule of law; it is only the exercises within that structure that often fail to adjust to it. He can continue to say this, because that disproportion between form and content is possible in a way that disproportion between form and matter never is. That difference, however, remains silent.

The universe which Weinrib must speak of is no longer created, but constituted, in its being; no longer nature, but subjectivity, in its knowing; and no longer public, but social in Arendt's sense, coalescing public with private. Facing that, one's speech can go no further in appropriating reality than to claim that justice is binding in the way it is only so long as we keep it so constructed. And Weinrib does not leave this silent, that we could dismantle the distinction, or shift activities from one to the other side of it, while repeating his most characteristic insistence: that, while they remain, they are hermetically sealed from each other.

Rhetoric

The scholars and practitioners who are Weinrib's audience have no recall of justice in nature, and of virtue as the locale of normativity, except through the scorn of modern philosophers. But their recall of Kant and Hegel is intuitive, within a democratic ethos which requires that one constitute one's normativity for onself, or for one's own group. The silence which attends Weinrib's address cannot escape what must be said to make this audience understand, once he simultaneously moves to refresh their memories on distribution and transaction in Aristotle.

INTERPRETATION OF TEXTS IN CONTEXTS

This study has attempted to exercise a method for interpretation of texts which does justice to their status as texts. That is, it recognizes that their status as words lies among other words, facing upon things, and addressed before persons. The substantive upshot of this exercise is to uncover a lacuna surrounding Aristotle's words and, by its visibility, to identify how to say what needs to be said in order for Aristotle's text to acquire our fuller recognition.

NOTES

1. *Aristotelis Ethica Nicomachea.* ed. J. Bywater. (Oxonii e typographico Clarendoniano, 1892); 1962 reprint. Aristotle. *Nicomachean Ethics.* Trans. M. Ostwald. (Indianapolis: Bobbs-Merrill, 1962).

2. Ernest J. Weinrib, *The Idea of Private Law* (Cambridge MA: Harvard University Press, 1995).

3. *Thomae Aquinatis in decem libros Ethicorum Aristotelis ad Nicomachum exposition*, cura Raymundi M. Spiazzi. (Taurini: Marietta, 1949); Thomas Aquinas. *Commentary on the Nicomachean Ethics.* Trans. C. I. Litzinger. Chicago: Henry Regnery, 1964.

4. C. B. Gray, "Topoi in Summa: Virtual Justice as Determinant for Aquinas' Placement of Law." *International Journal for the Semiotics of Law* 19 (2006) 325–338.

CHAPTER SIX

FREEDOM AND NECESSITY IN ST. ANSELM'S *CUR DEUS HOMO*

> Ideo enim necessitate fuerant quia futura erant; et futura erant, quia fuerunt; et fuerunt, quia fuerunt . . . . Scito omnia ex necessitate fuisse, quia ipse voluit. Voluntatem vero eius nulla praecessit necessitas[1]

> For therefore were [all the things undertaken by Christ] necessary, because they were to be, and they were to be because they were, and they were because they were . . . . Know that they were of necessity because he wished them to be. But no necessity preceded his will.[2]

SYNTACTICS

Syntax renders intelligible the first part of this citation. The events in question possess the modality of impossibility for non-occurrence. From the speaker's viewpoint (time 1) they possess this modality at some prior temporal location (time 2). Time 2 is also prior to some other assumed point (time 3) prior to time 1. The non-modal presence or affirmability of the events at time 3 is taken to be the necessity for their modal presence at time 2, i.e., if the first is not present then neither will be the second.

Secondly, the presence at time 3 has its necessity in the presence of the events at a time 4 still prior to time 3. This time 4 seems to coincide in the argument with time 3, time 3 being that point with respect to time 2, and time 4 being that same point with respect to time 1.

Finally, the presence at time 4 is said to have no further necessity among events of the same kind, i.e., those which could be replacements for the events in question. Instead, the second part of our original statement shows that will is the only necessity for the events. The necessity residing in the events is will, but there is no event in time such that this will is necessary.

Thus the passage states that the order of dependence runs as follows from the unnecessary to the necessary: (0→) will → non-modal presence at time 3–4 → necessity at time 2 → necessity at time 1.

SEMANTICS: INTERPRETATION

Grammar: Chapter 18a

The immediate surroundings of the text in chapter eighteen are the discussions of events of Christ's life, and the will of Christ as making necessary those events. Once this solution has been stated, the conclusion follows that Christ met death without being necessitated to do so. This appears as an intermediate conclusion to the intention of the whole work. It is not the only possible way in which the events could have been related; but it is a sufficient explanation and satisfactory. This is a reasonable explanation for Anselm, but this does not suffice to make it absolutely certain in his eyes, for God may do things impenetrable to reason. This will render reason as not the ultimate criterion for what is the state of affairs and what is not. This solution is a choice among many possibilities, not all of which may be available to human knowing.

The text is preceded in this chapter by the reference to Aristotle's doctrine of subsequent necessity, which apparently destroys choice together with choosable alternatives. Subsequent necessity, however, is inoperative and simply a restatement of the fact itself, that a fact is a fact. It does not equal or demand a causal necessity, called antecedent necessity.

Anselm exemplifies such antecedent causal necessity by the movement of the heavens; they revolve because they must revolve. This is more than saying they must revolve because they are revolving. In the context of speaking of Aristotle's doctrine of necessity, then, Anselm introduces the Aristotelian example of necessary movement but now calls it antecedent necessity. It is sure that Aristotle, while distinguishing between events which did and those which did not have a particular kind of necessity, would never have said that behind the movement of the heavens was unconditioned choice. Anselm surely is unjust to Aristotelian doctrine in claiming that he destroys alternatives and (simply) ascribes necessity to all things; but he is right insofar as the will which Anselm places antecedent to factual necessity has no place for Aristotle. There was necessity of more than mere fact to the revolution of the heavens for Aristotle, but no antecedent necessity, no prior will. The necessity Aristotle saw is left in by Anselm, but its position is not ultimate.

Anselm precedes the discussion of antecedent necessity in this chapter with some notes on the relation of constancy and freedom. One does not lose freedom when he persists in a decision made freely at first, even if he has to be forced into this compliance. Choice rather than determination is the antithesis of necessity.

This is the explanation for our usage of attributing necessity to God, e.g., in regard to his perfections. The necessity does not inhere in God, as though depriving him of his free choice for good, but rather inheres in the non-divine agent which finds itself incapable of altering divine free choice. Interference is impossible, i.e., non-interference is necessary to the finite being. So in regard to altering the subsequent necessity of a past fact, God should not be called impotent but rather the fact should be called incapable of altering God's free choice which is the antecedent necessity of that fact.

The message of chapter eighteen in regard to the previous syntactical analysis could be stated so: divine will is the source of necessity at time 2, but the necessity at time 2 is not retroactive upon its source.

Grammar: The Work

To appreciate the statements here, we must next see their place in the sequence of the whole work.. The passage with which we are working comes near the end of one of the final chapters in the latter of two books, designed to provide the Christian with answers to the infidel supported by reason alone. The first book proves the impossibility of man's salvation without Christ, and the second proves how it is possible for Christ to save men. The basic problem running throughout the nearly fifty chapters is that to which chapter eighteen has offered a comprehensive answer, viz., how God could be man, and for such a purpose, without contradiction of his divine nature. This is the query of the infidels to whom this is addressed. In lieu of examining each chapter in sequence for points bearing upon our locus' freedom-necessity, divine-human, action-nature relationships, only the central problems and the possible answers given, which surround the chapter in question, will be examined.

The root problem is how God can become man without taking on various characterizations which the divine nature excludes. There are several parries to this thrust, as when Anselm lets these imperfections slide off the divine onto Christ as man (I, 8), or such as his counter to the charge that God must punish dishonor by saying that only among men does the dishonor take place and that the need for vengeance is only for the edification of men (I, 14–15). But the charges are also taken frontally in several situations, in each one by a reduction of the apparent necessity to a root of free choice. Christ needed not die, but only be just, as a consequence of which he was persecuted; that is, his death was the result of a choice to be holy rather than being its condition (I, 9). Even where the free choice is not apparent, it can still be presumed present; for one chooses something as long as he does not choose something else which would preclude the first (I, 9). What necessity there is, is not the most basic structure, because it is the consequence solely of a free creation (II, 5).

Yet, for all this, we remain perplexed; and justly so for Anselm, since the redemption is a much more apparently contradictory affair than the creation, a much greater deed (II, 16). Despite all the reduction to will, it still holds true that the will of God is a sufficient reason only because it is never irrational (I, 8); that there is no liberty except for the best and the fitting (I, 12); that nothing is haphazard for God (I, 16). And at the very end, just before the text from which we began, Anselm finally admits to Boso that some reason must be shown for the divine act, lest total disbelief ensue. He then proceeds to tell a story, and concludes that the condition for speech about God, the ultimate, must be whatever is fitting and uncontradicted, and that this will be necessary of God (II, 16)—a conclusion long since rejected by claiming that the fit could only work as an adornment to the necessary instead of supplying for it (I, 4).

Then follows our text, which tries to solve the same problem by distinguishing kinds of necessity and claiming, again, only one kind for the events of Christ's life.

Finally, following this, is the conclusion that, in alternative goods, the better among them is defined only by free will; the better is a function of choice rather than a preliminary to choice. The only obligation one has is to do as he chooses (II, 18b). Presumed throughout this is that the alternatives are present and neutrally good, so that choice will have play for its creations. Presumably, this is always the case for God; but what is the explanation for God's freedom before the good-or-bad, rather than just the good-or-good? It is precisely as distinguishing the good and bad that the will can be holy (II, 1). Here again the indecision of Anselm appears; he affirms his conclusion on the grounds of what a God must be, in order to be a God, but cannot himself reach the demonstration that *his* God is such.

Grammar: History

The difficulties from which Anselm believes to have extricated himself but which might appear to as yet unsolved by him may so appear because we are using non-Anselmian norms to judge Anselm's argument. This is the question of the position *of Cur Deus Homo*, and of our text from book two, chapter eighteen, In particular, within the history of philosophy. This perspective may be partially explored now, but some of it will be left until discussion of the rhetoric of the work as the key to the passage.

The underlying belief throughout the work is that necessity is antithetical to the divine; the most divine characteristic is not inalienable rest, as for the Aristotelian self-contemplating mover; nor is it unavoidable self-development in Plotinian manner. It is difficult to specify just what it is that is divine about God. His perfection is to remain constant, but not necessarily so; he must remain free, but not self-contradictorily so. For this God, his will itself is the only limit—but it is a real limit. The formula of interpretation seems to be that the description of God is a function of our estimation of the best and most perfect, that whatever is most perfect cannot be lacking in God. If God wishes something ungodlike, we do not presume it is thus right but rather that the willer could not have been God (I, 12). It is impossible to attribute anything in the least unbecoming to God (I,

10). Under such a principle, whatever we find as best in ourselves we must place in God, even if it is hard to reconcile some of these perfections. Notice that, contrary to Xenophanes, it is not the human that is made the divine, but rather the divine that is in the human is divinely predicated.

What kind of God must this be? He will be one who takes thought for his creatures, In fact, more thought in saving them than in creating them (II, 16). Care is found to be a divine characteristic of men, and so a characteristic of the divine. Boso is startled when Anselm shows that God is owed a debt by us for stealing his honor. What startles, if not that such interests would seem at first sight rather ungodly for a deity, in terms of theology as the philosophers have seen it—the escape from fear with the pedant-god of Aristotle, the do-nothing deities of Epicurus, the co-op divinity of Plotinus. The nearest approach to Anselm's conception is the Arab lawgiver-god; but this god, ill-harmonized with his Aristotelian model, finds his moral function to be simply a threat over the terrestial affairs of men, who were the ones who needed morality rather than god needing it. Anselm's God comes close to this conception insofar as God cannot be dishonored in himself, with the locus of such disorder being the order and beauty of the universe, as related to man, not to God (I, 14–15). But Anselm's God is truly a punisher of evil because he can take note of the events of men's morality and be interested therein, whereas for Averroes it would be difficult to see God as taking such positive action. The Anselmian God can act among men because of his care for them, and he has care for them because care is a perfection for men to have among themselves and God can be lacking in nothing which is good for men.

This possibility for care and consideration appears again, for both men and gods, when Anselm affirms that "no advantage one has apart from choice constitutes happiness" (II, 12). This would parallel the words of Critias that nature is no rewarder, that reward is a creation of men and dependent on their choice. But the "nature" and the "creation" are different here, such that Anselm in this view of freedom and necessity resembles more Antiphon the Sophist in his plaint that the freedom of the city is a fetter, that the freedom of nature is the only true happiness. Yet here, too, Anselm is reducible to neither of the perspectival extremes, despite surface similarities; he stands in a different perspective, where freedom or choice is not nature and yet is not convention. Choice, and the deliberation which precedes it and is possible only because the possibility for choice is present, becomes irreducible to anything more ultimate than itself.

God does not lose his self-sufficiency by his ability to choose and man does not gain the ability to choose by his self-sufficiency. The ideal of self-sufficiency is retained from Aristotle and most of the philosophers, and is used in such a way as to demand that man recover his own salvation and self-sufficiency, since it was the man Adam who lost it (II, 8); here the ideal is apparent. But, on the other hand, self-sufficiency is doom forever, as it was for the sinful angels; man can be saved only because he was weak and not self-sufficient, being set upon by powers stronger than himself to plot his fall (II, 21). This position would seem to mean that man is adequate and self-controlled in willing, but not in knowing; this interpretation is supported by the fact that some choices are impossible because we know too much and that only ignorance would allow that act to take place (II, 15).

In terms of such primacy of will in God, and in man, for Anselm, what effects will this historical context have upon our vision of the text with which our discussion deals? When Anselm says *voluntatem vero eius nulla praecessit necessitas*, this is a new word. None of the Greek philosophers have spoken thus, because it would have rendered God unknowable even to himself. Necessity, however, followed upon his will and is the condition for the knowledge of God. God can be known in the subsequent necessities of his will, but he cannot be known beyond this into some prior condition for his will: *fuerunt quia fuerunt*, Thus, Anselm's explanation is hypothetical or possible; it does not exclude alternative reasons, although the same condition must be present at the conclusion. The basic truth is a truth of God; the ways of arriving at it may be taken as inconsequential. Thus, if the thing sought is the same, though some appeal because they do not believe and some because they do (I, 2), then those who do not should be able to be convinced, even of this divine mystery.

RHETORIC

The broadest characterization of this work is, of course, as dialogue. The significance of this broad genre will be left aside until the more specific relationships of voice and address have been studied.

The most immediate relationship, and that which mediates all the others, is that between the characters Anselm and Boso in the dialogue. The two are pictured as acquaintances, with the relation of mentor and disciple. Boso requests Anselm to speak at the beginning and has to urge him to do so; later on, however, Anselm at his own initiative continues when Boso is satisfied (I. 16). Boso has the role of instigating the questions, and also of answering Anselm when the latter is responding and eliciting assent or dissent to his response. The more objections Anselm resolves, the more deeply the underlying grounds of that resolution appear to Boso as problematic; Anselm is the condition for Boso's seeing more problems; and Boso's view of the problems is the condition for Anselm's resolution. At times Boso falters and has to have Anselm bring forth the difficulties himself, while at other times Anselm must be urged to continue. The problems would not appear and would not be resolved unless both were present.

From this immediacy of discussion the representative functions of the two figures may be studied. For besides these two disputants in the *Cur Deus Homo*, Anselm the writer of this dialogue also appears in his own person, talking to his readers at the beginning of both of the two books, and in the preface to the whole. And at the end of the second book, the Anselm-disputant seems to be speaking for Anselm-writer. What is the relationship of the two Anselms? .Anselm introduces his work with reference to his exile and the subsequent lack of leisure to polish the books. He stresses that both books proceed as if without revelation, and that the divisions of both are to be kept intact lest something be lost. In the first chapter Anselm-writer tells his reason for the dialogue form, viz., to make the investigation available to all, even the less witful. Its purpose is to set the understanding at ease.

Anslem-writer, then, uses Anselm-disputant as a tool for better accomplishing the writer's purpose. Anselm-disputant should be fully under the control of Anselm-writer (as, in fact, should Boso). Yet this is certainly not the case. For, as mentioned above, the Anselm-disputant is involved with Boso in such a way that the dialogue, whatever it would be, would at least not be the same without both parties present. Anselm-disputant is not solely under the control of Anselm-writer, but also under that of Boso. But is not Boso also a product of Anselm-writer's mind? True, at least in part; but this is not the same as saying that Anselm-disputant says the same thing as Anselm-writer. He is only a part of what the writer would say; if nothing else, he is the writer brought to us through the medium of-another, rather than the writer immediately present.

Yet Anselm-disputant certainly is closer to the thought of Anselm-writer than is Boso; Boso is a tool of negation and privation whereby a vacuum is shown which the writer, through his speaker, can fill up. So Anselm-disputant is identified with Anselm-writer in a stronger sense. When the disputant rebukes Boso (I, 16), it is the writer doing so; when Anselm-disputant declares a digression to have done no harm (I. 18), again it is the writer's opinion. But when this happens, it is also the writer rebuking part of his own thought, or excusing the excuser. The dialogue going on in the play is the same as that in the playwright.

Thus the objections are not just those of an alien, but belong to Anselm the man as well. And the difficulties in understanding for which the dialogue form was found necessary in the first chapter, are not only someone else's difficulties, but the author's. The dialogue is for the enlightenment of not just the common reader; it is also for that of the author. Because the problem is "plain to all in the solution", Anselm cannot realize how "very difficult in the investigation" this is except through some alienated aspect of himself (I, 1).

The third dimension in this rhetorical analysis is on the side of Boso, who makes himself the representative of confused Christians and ridiculing infidels, i.e., from Jewry and Islam. Boso himself believes, yet cannot see around the rational contradictions which are the excuse for the infidels' non-belief. He will stand in the tension of having to know just where his pose ends and doubt begins. His belief is not sheer contemplation of truth, then; he must seek penetration of reason. What will this penetration be? In terms of the problem presented by the infidels, reason is antithetical to contradiction, and the contradiction here is that God can be God and have ungodly characteristics (weakness, injustice, necessitation, imprudence, wastefulness). The penetration will show either that no contradiction exists here or else that the alleged ungodly characteristics are not, in fact, present in God, thus dissolving the contradiction. What one ends with, then, is the possibility or non-impossibility of a God doing what the Christians claim he did. The antagonists here are both believers in the scripture of the old law, apparently, since Anselm claims to be speaking in a non-revealed context and yet presumes many of the doctrines of the genesis and fall in his statements.

The conclusions here are supposed to be necessary, yet one questions whether or not they were intended to demonstrate the faith. This is a question of the relation between Anselm and his dialogue with us his readers. As Christians we are enlightened; as unbelievers it appears that he would wish to prove to us the truths of faith. But demonstration refers to reason, that which is a different referent from belief. Insofar as this goes, what we should come out with is minimally a conviction of the non-contradictoriness of Christian belief in the God-man. But because the dialogue is carried on between a believer and a believer, one of whom takes a role of doubt (one aspect of Anselm) and the other of whom takes a role of belief (another Anselm), the faith which cannot be demonstrated but only cleared away for, will have much more chance to take root. The end of the argument is not the *ergo* of a thesis but the conviction of a hearer who, like us, does not have every point proven nor expects to, but who nonetheless believes. Because the final reaction is a human one and not a computerized one, there is a higher likelihood that Anselm's speech to us his readers will be more effective. This guide for the perplexed Christian does not pretend to dissolve religious faith philosophically, to reduce it to philosophy.

The final dimension of the dialogue relation is the place of God who speaks to Anselm-writer, Anselm-disputant, the antagonist Boso, and the readers. We do not know in what way he has spoken to Anselm-writer; perhaps there is a clue in saying that right order requires us to believe the deep things of Christian faith before we undertake to discuss them by reason (I, 2). To Boso God speaks through Anselm; but Anselm speaks to himself through Boso.

Carrying out the point made above, this will mean that God comes through both of them to Anselm-writer. Anselm must speak in order to know or learn from God, and he must know from God before he can speak of God and his philosophical justification. Anselm only shows what God has given him, and God gives himself freely to Anselm when Anselm gives freely of himself in discussion (I, 1–2).

In this light, then, what significance does our text take on? The dependence of all necessity upon the will of God is not only the situation in regard to the facts of Christ's life. It also holds true of the discussion of these facts, and of any discussion. The necessity. of Anselm's discourse comes to it only because it is in dialogue; and only because it is in dialogue, i.e., where Anselm is giving of himself freely, is God speaking to him. The truth of human knowledge comes from the giver of all good gifts, and this giver reveals himself between men. Rather than some other means, e.g., impersonal demonstration, the subjective communication has a much greater likelihood of obtaining its desired result precisely because its mode gives a greater opportunity for God's insertion of himself. The Anselmian perspective takes seriously "where love abides, God is there".

The dialogue form in use here is not the Ciceronian mutual juxtaposition of views. It is like the Platonic, being an instrument of resolution rather than eclecticism; but it differs in that the common is not the area wherein what truth is reveals itself so much as reveals himself, thus rectifying the personification which affects the Platonic ideas in their self-sharing as much as it affects Aristotle's nature in its self-realization. The perspective is more Augustinian insofar as truth is a Self-revelation discovered in a self-revelation, with the difference that now the realization comes in the precariousness of mutual control rather than in the manageability of meditation.

Logic

The need to coordinate subject matter with presentation, to make one live up to the other, is recognized at the very beginning, where Anselm-disputant hesitates because of the danger that a poor rhetoric might not only embarrass the stylist but also reflect upon the subject as well, dissuading the disappointed from it. Instead, this the most beautiful object must be treated in the most gracious manner.

That will never do for the grandstands, says Boso. What they want is hard, cold reason, whose necessity mimics the necessity of the subject's connections (I, 4). Anselm agrees to use the best he has, and proceeds to do so.

But he does not get very far. From that start it is sure that ever deeper grounds lie hidden beyond anything we can say or know (I, 2). If this is so, then the demonstration might not just fail to include those reasons, but might positively exclude them, while remaining an apparent demonstration; the net result must be that demonstration is always falsifiable—by the-authority who *knows* (I, 2; I, 18). For instance, philosophers, working from what was apparently apodictic, have never considered even the possibility that man might not be by nature and essence mortal in body. But revelation shows that there is a better than even chance that he was never meant to die (II, 11). The value of philosophy is to point out some reason, any at all, so that by the appearance of one reason the listener may come to believe that there may be yet deeper ones; but if no reason were attempted, then no reason would be suspected by another (II, 16). This is not a useless flight of fancy in divine science, for concerning God we can presume nothing unfit and so even the smallest reason has the weight of necessity as long as it is not overbalanced by a greater one (I, 10). If something is more fit, and no further objection can be made for its application to God, then it is necessary (II, 16).

Yet because the better does not bind over the good but is a function of the will (II, 18b), this necessity can never become apodictic. To return to our working text: will is the condition for necessity; and the only necessity relative to God is subsequent necessity totally dependent on will, i.e., facts—facts to which man does not have immediate access because Christ always retains a higher wisdom which does not appear before men (II, 13). By himself, man has but principles, the conditions of possibility for facts. How can men gain access to Christ's higher wisdom? Only when God gives it freely. When and where does God give this freely? When man gives freely of himself: In dialogue.

Thus far the formal logic of the work. The material logic which this principle of access through dialogue maps is the incarnate Christ. Man's only escape from sin must lie beyond the totality of his own self and of all created things (I, 20–21). But God became man because God cannot toil while Christ as man can (I, 8). As any man, Christ the God-man can have no good or holy will except from God; Christ's will is derived from his divinity, not from his humanity (I, 9). In return, Christ offers up his humanity to his divinity; he offers himself in his own honor (II, 18b).

This is the parallel: the essence of God's honor lies in visibility (I, 14–15), i.e., primarily in Christ; and man's reconciliation, on the other hand, is possible only because he exists in communion with others rather than in the grand self-sufficiency of the irredeemable angels (II, 21). The two movements meet in this dialogue, which discovers the interworking of the human and divine, Christ the God-man, through the interworking of the human—Anselm and Boso, who purvey the believer's and the disbeliever's reasoning, respectively, but who also respectively render philosophical (human) answers to the believer's (divinely inspired) faith. The material logic becomes even clearer when we remember that Anselm and Boso, though distinct points of view, remain somehow but one, i.e., Anselm-writer. Anselm's dialectic towards salvation in the public arena is the model of the Christ's dialectic among men in saving them. Anselm's dialectic (the rhetoric) is the possibility (as first for us) of reaching Christ's; but Christ's dialectic (the grammar) is the possibility (as first in itself) for performing Anselm's successfully, since redemption is even more difficult than creation, which could be done alone.

If this is the logic of the whole, it ought to apply to the parts, including that text upon which this chapter tries to focus. This does appear to be so, for the text claims to state the total contingency of all necessity upon the free choice of God; but at the end of the chapter (as divided in the 1946 Latin edition, not the Open Court English translation), Anselm reneges from promising further discussion with Boso because of the uncertainties of future events. Any future encounter is commended to the will of God, as indeed it must be if the principles stated in our small text are correct.

PRAGMATICS: RETRORSION

The remaining task is to discover how the four lines of Anselm are claimed to be interpreted into our preceding dozen some pages. The two writings are certainly not the same writing. The present one has not said all that Anselm's did, nor has Anselm's said all that this one has. What was missing from Anselm's was a treatment of itself; what is missing from this one is any interest in proving or disproving the original topic. The subject of this one has been the treatment of the original topic rather than that topic itself. This treatment is like Anselm's, however, in that it does not focus upon itself, until now.

Here the principles of evidence upon which the preceding part rested may be laid out. In the second part this author looked at a text which appeared in its meaning through the media of several surpassing contexts—those of matter and mode and their relation. The justification for the alleged interpretation is identical with these contexts; but the text itself is not something apart from these contexts but is rather what makes them its context by its presence within them as something other than them. The objective of the second part was to state what is implied if the text objectified by the first part is to take on the meaning which it does have. These are not stated by the original text but only implied, for the possibilities for choice of alternatives appear only when the whole of the work, history and rhetoric are explicitated; but even this grasp of the "self-contained" meaning will depend upon the more general possibilities offered by the reader's comprehension of the composition-language as a set of prior alternatives which can be expanded only through the instrumentality of those same alternatives. The stretching out of these alternatives, not in precisely their contrariety but in the universe of discourse embracing both contraries as harmonized or bypassed in terms of their container or principle of differentiation, is the task of the second part, just as it was of the first part in relation to the original four lines. The task of this part, then, must be the same, i.e., to state the conditions of possibility of the second part.

How can the conditions of possibility and of justification for the second part be assessed? If one is able to state those conditions now it will only be because the second is finished. To write those conditions in the course of writing that part would have justified what was not yet present to be justified. The first condition for the second part qua commentary or justification is that there be something prior to it which is completed as an unjustified whole. Only when this takes its place among other writings which cannot write about themselves until written is there a place at all which is capable of being written about. The first principle underlying the interpretation in part two is that there must be some stage of completion before the possibility for continuation (interpretation) occurs. The content may or may not be important for the task, but the temporal stage surely is.

If this is the first principle, the next will be the specification of continuation. To continue there must be a remaining .presence or else there would be unprecedented beginning. To continue there must be the absence of something that is relinquished or else there would be specific identity of texts. To write the second part about the text, there must be something of but not all of the text remaining. What that portion of the text remaining will be, will not be a physical portion but an aspect thereupon, i.e., a consideration which is not contained in the text but, qua consideration, is added by the commentator. Ultimately there is more of the new than of the old in the interpretation, since even what remains .remains only mediately, i.e., as already interpreted. With this recognized, there is no apparent limit to the divergence which an interpretation of the text could make and still remain an interpretation. That is to say, relative to the first principle, the original of the text is quite over and done.

These are principles allowing interpretation; what allows precisely philosophical interpretation? The completion must be completely complete, the.divergence must be devastating yet just thereby so much the more embracing of the remnants. In doing so the conditions of ultimacy itself are put into question. This is the endeavor which, unavoidably, the author must have had in the second part; yet he is now interpreting that part. The conditions for final justification and final possibility will be the same as the less ultimate conditions, i.e., prior completion and a remaining absent existence thereof. Everything must be done and finished and packed away in any obvious sense; and the only completedness of all possibility lies in the principle of that completedness, its condition of possibility. Then we need not claim that such a condition is present to be brought into focus, since that which it allows is not present and the presence of that principle would be functionless.

But if in its entirety not all has been said, been completed, and the penultimate interpretation has not been made, yet it has been made in its actual possibility, what can be said has been said. The immediately preceding sentence did so. It can be named, and though not knowing that material we yet know its blueprint, what it must be if this name is to apply. And what the final condition must be is that about which nothing further can be said, that is to say, that which cannot be interpreted. It can take part in no proposition but must lie outside—whether prior or posterior or even unrelated to—of the cosmos of propositions. Yet it has been stated.

To go further and state the condition for stating the unstatable is again to attempt to state that which is in principle unstatable in principle: meaning by its own principle, by itself, not by spoken principle. To transfer this from the universe of logical demands to the psychological correlates will yield a faculty at once under limitations yet going beyond them, i.e., both necessary and free, both contemplative and active. ("[W]hen a creature wishes to do a thing that is left entirely at his own disposal, we say that he *ought* to do it . . . freed from all obligations *except* to do as he chose." II, 18b; my emphasis) But this ability does not differentiate its two directions in a separable manner, as, e.g., one a necessitated faculty, and another but free faculty; rather both are one, just as the logical demand plus the impotency. Only fidelity renders intelligible the ultimate part of the statement preceding. How *must* I while I *can't*? No worry: "no necessity preceded his will," the text tells us.

NOTES

1. S. Anselmi Cantuariensis Archiepiscopi *Omnia opera*, 6 vols., ed. Franciscus Salesius Schmitt (Edinburg: Thomas Nelson, 1946), vol. 2, p. 125; II, 18a, ad finem.

2. St. Anselm, *Basic Writings*, trans. S. N. Deane, 2nd ed. (La Salle IL: Open Court, 1964), p. 277. All later references are to this translation.

CHAPTER SEVEN

BONAVENTURE'S PROOF OF TRINITY

This chapter is an attempt to show that Bonaventure did not foreclose a proof by reason alone for the existence of God as triune. This attempt will center in the argument Bonaventure presents in his early work, the *Commentary on the Sentences*, in particular the third distinction of its first book[1]. It is here that the only time Bonaventure explicitly raises this question occurs. It is here, also, that he appears to answer it decisively in the negative.

This is not Bonaventure's only approach to the question of proving the existence of God. In other settings, however, the proof concerns God as supreme being, not as triune. This is, for example, the direction of his passage in the *Mystery of the Trinity* which has been offered undergraduates for forty years in the Wippel and Wolter anthology, however innovative that proof might be in other respects[2]. Nonetheless, Bonaventure's more characteristic approach to godhead is to a triune being, so that proof of supreme being is for him far from a proof of what truly exists. While trinity is the mainstream Christian belief, it is the Bonaventurian passion.

Theologians have recovered passion for trinity, in a way that compels them to work philosophically upon trinity, as well. If Christian theology takes as its focus the reality of God, not a defective substitute, and that reality is triune, then trinity is its focus. But the same will then be true for non-Christian religions (Viladesau)[3] and for the non-religious exercise of philosophy. If these, too, are authentic approaches to the reality of God, they also will be approaches to trinity, for it is the very nature of God to be related (LaCugna, 177; Hill, 1987, 410; Zabzebski, 15) (3).

The theological recovery of trinity has been through reappreciating revelation. To Christians, God's expression to humans is God, not something else, not some set of words; "God speaks his own being" (Williams, 206). But for this sort of expression to be possible externally, to humans or in creation, "in the structure of revelation" (Lash 190), it must occur immanently as well, within trinity (Fisher, 524; Leinsle, 14).

One problem from identifying "immanent" trinity with the "economic" trinity, with God as known by visible works, whether of revelation or of creation, is that creation then appears to be as necessary an event as the immanent relation is (O'Donnell, 155, 164; Hankey; Reichberg). Deduction of trinity from the fact of revelation, and conceiving God as incomplete without an engagement in creation and liberation, has been answered in terms of trinity itself. This is done in one way by stressing the finitude of any personal distinction even within trinity (Keane, 64), its "difference" and otherness (Milbank, 215); thus the difference of creation lies already within its source. Another way has been to stress the fullness in the category of the personal, so that necessitation fits with personal procession no more than it does with the act of creation (Hill, 1986, 397; Clark 1992).

Reinstating persons-in-relation as a primary metaphysical category is an avenue for theorists of social analogy. For them, tritheism loses some of its unacceptability when loyalty among the persons cannot be divided (Layman, 294; Martinisch; Purcell; contrary to Swinburne, see Alston, Forrest), or at least it is found preferable to the contradiction within what is conceived as its sole alternative, the relative tritheism in which only some sortals are numerically distinct among persons, while others are not (Bartel 131–3).

These solutions to the revelatory impasses of trinity solve anew the older problem of explaining the freedom in creation: if plenitude of goodness overflows into creation, must it not do so necessarily, and interminably? The responses are, again, that finitude already is rooted in goodness by the non-identity of trinity (Keane, 64) ; and, even more, that any demand for the boundless expression of goodness is fully satisfied within trinity, without there needing to be creation in order for this to be satisfied (Cousins, 74).

These novel solutions require some rethinking also within the history of trinitarian thought. This is done partly by upgrading an Eastern stress upon threeness in preference to the Western primacy given to unity. But, to balance that research, language on the one hand is rediscovered to have little room for multiplicity in the use of any ascriptions at all, even the ascription of person (Plantigna, 335; Bartel, 152). On the other side, Augustine's attention to immanent unity, even in his psychological analogy which Bonaventure will be seen to inherit, is found not to be as exhaustive as is claimed (LaCugna, 76; Milbank 214; Rezende; Lancaster), and is discovered to have appeared only late in his career (Clark, 76) In turn, while Anselm is on the one hand taxed for substantializing the persons (Milbank, 215; Hankey), he is as well perceived to have recognized the possibility for the rational demonstration of trinity which this study will be testing.

Thomas denied that this demonstration is possible, since the act of creation is attributed to the divine persons commonly, in their unity. No signs of trinity, then, appear in the created effect, whereby trinity can be inferred (Viladesau, 321; Emory 1996, 2000; Kretzmann, 25, citing *S. Th.* I, 32, 1, c.). Another version of this is that trinitarian relations do not occur in time, and so cannot leave evidence there (Milbank, 216), overlooking that they continue to occur throughout time. The recent stress upon trinity as the concrete reality of godness provides the response to this: the perfection of the cause of a reality, and not only as partialled out into its aspects, is what appears in the effect. Differently put, subjectivity underlies causality (Hill, 1986, 387). Trinitarian vestiges may be differently perceived now—the three domains of human experiencing (Kern, 35), some three dimensions of historic reasoning (Darcus, 177), for example among Whiteheadean or Derridean moves (Bracken; Sanders)—but searching for them is perhaps even better founded now.

EXEMPLARITY OF TRINITY BY IMAGES

Wherever else than the *Commentary* that Bonaventure's topic is trinity, as in the *Mystery*, *Itinerarium*,_*Reductio* and *Collationes*, it is not the rational proof for trinity that is addressed, but only the analysis and the meaningfulness of trinity, in itself and for humans' return to God. His preoccupation appears in his metaphysics' concern with emanation, exemplarity and reduction. These three dynamics are trinity's life in the world, such that created realities bear the marks of trinity from their creation, show those marks so that trinity can be recognized from them, and supply those marks as the route to reaching life in God. Particularly the exemplarity occurs in the context of an accepted principle of causation, namely, that the effect can have no more perfection than its cause, so its perfections will manifest those of its cause, with whatever coefficient of error their differences may import (51A). While Bonaventure is willing to design the *Commentary* around the four Aristotelean causes, he names this causal process, exemplary cause.

This is the philosophical tool which allows for the rational approach to truths of faith. Bonaventure finds ample scope for this activity: to refute skeptics, to strengthen believers and to give delight to strong believers (9B). Bonaventure is not concerned with the ontologism by which natural knowledge of trinity is sometimes declaimed; for he constantly distinguishes the knowledge of God as God is, which is true and accurate, from the complete, adequate and exhaustive knowledge of God made possible only by sharing the nature of God (49A, passim, for example).

The commonplace as to Bonaventure's proof for the existence of God is that he finds this proof unnecessary if not impossible. Because God's existence is contuited, any proofs are at best ratiocinations, "no more and"—note—"no less" than dialectical exercises to confirm our realization of God's existence (Hellman, 112, Scapin, 149; Dewan; Seifert; Charron and Doyle). For the person in grace, they are not needed; for the person resisting grace, they are not possible. These commonplaces are updated by authors' redescription of Bonaventure as a difference-theorist and a deconstructionist of Aristotelean texts (Mackey,

57); philosophers, who fail to understand the created text aright (Leinsle), are dyslexic rather than just sinners. The extent of their intention to confirm this ideological imposition textually can be appreciated from the overview that " 'Bonaventure' is not a proper name, but a synecdoche for revealed religion." (Mackey, 57; Pieretti).

These commonplaces might appear to rule out in advance any discussion about the soundness of some particular argument or another, the very discussion in this study. But the contrary is true, in fact. Even if demonstrations about the existence of the one godhead were outlawed, those regarding trinity might not be, since they are no longer about abstractions, but about reality. As well, for the most part there is no attempt to show that Bonaventure does not take the proofs he proffers as demonstrative ones, only that he does not need them. They may be demonstrative regardless of this, especially since the contuited knowledge is only habitual and undifferentiated, not full and actual (Leinsle, 149). And, indeed, the most likely statements of the commonplace even admit that the demonstrations are fully correct (Beuchot, 316; Fedoryka; Landston).

The argument can be made more strongly, however: that not only is proof unnecessary for Bonaventure, but that demonstrative natural theology cannot reach what is distinctively Christian and revealed (Kretzman, 15). Or even that Aristotelean demonstration is "essentially deceptive" in Bonaventure's eyes (Mackay, 44). Even more would that view rule out the literal reading of his argument which this study gives. So Bonaventure's attitude toward Aristotelean philosophy as a whole requires some comment.

Bonaventure's preference for Aristotle over Plato is remarked, since Plato makes knowledge impossible (Russo, 60). Even Bonaventure's aprioristic argument for godness is taken as more Aristotelean, since Bonaventure's "Seinshymnus"—if God is God, God is—demands multiplicity, while Parmenides' "Seinsvampyr" devours singularity (Wagner,39; Aersen). Bonaventure and his school are noted for their preference toward dealing with Aristotle's own texts, rather than with the interpretations by Arab commentators (Scala, 554).

Bonaventure's categories for analysis—mode, species and number, for starters—differ from Aristotle's (Leinsle, 63); but they are categories for analysis all the same. Conventional Aristotelean predication may appear to Augustine, Bonaventure's model, as inadequate to handle godtalk; but unconventional and still Aristotelean predication is up to the task (Rudebusch, 596, citing *Meta.* 7.3, 1029a 23–24; Barbone; Bowman).

The most severe complaint has to do with predication in the category of substance, however. While Aristotle's logic deals with substances and their causes as self-contained ontic data, and as the normal states of being, Christian logic must see them as dependent, and as in a fallen and temporary state of being (Mackey, 48, 55; Bowman, 11). Bonaventure himself, however, cannot fail to see that nothing is a pure sign, a function without substance; creation of substance, of existences with a relative autonomy, is the condition both for there being anything at all to serve as signs, and especially any thing to serve as signs of the autonomous relations in their triune cause. As well, this misses one distinctiveness of the Franciscan school (e.g., De Boni), if the critics think that Bonaventure is attached to either an unfallen world or the fallen one, rather than to a world already redeemed and restored, i.e., a world which is in principle already back into or past its normal state forever.

The same critic, in fact, reinstates for Bonaventure a more Aristotelean epistemology and science when he insists elsewhere upon the inseparability of each created universal from its created individuals. While this is manifestly the core Aristotelean position, it is also what is seen as both the distinctive Franciscan posture and, remarkably, the best imaging of oneness and threeness in trinity (Mackey, 1979, 134).

Exemplifying Features of Images

There is not only one set of marks left by trinitarian creation upon things of the world. Nothing is easier than to look at everything in threes . . . or fours, or twos. Bonaventure inherits substances and their causes as self-contained ontic data, and as the normal states of being, Christian logic must see them as dependent, and as in a fallen and temporary state of being (Mackey, 48, 55; Bowman, 11). Bonaventure himself, however, cannot fail to see that nothing is a pure sign, a function without substance; creation of substance, of existences with a relative autonomy, is the condition both for there being anything at all to serve as signs, and especially any thing to serve as signs of the autonomous relations in their triune cause. As well, this misses one distinctiveness of the Franciscan school, if the critics think that Bonaventure is attached to either an unfallen world or the fallen one, rather than to a world already redeemed and restored, i.e., a world which is in principle already back into or past its normal state forever.

The same critic, in fact, reinstates for Bonaventure a more Aristotelean epistemology and science when he insists elsewhere upon the inseparability of each created universal from its created individuals. While this is manifestly the core Aristotelean position, it is also what is seen as both the distinctive Franciscan posture and, remarkably, the best imaging of oneness and threeness in trinity (Mackey, 1979, 134).

Exemplary Arguments from Images

What Bonaventure argues in the first part of distinction three is that the trace of trinity in worldly beings is insufficient to demonstrate the existence of divine trinity, and in the second article of the second part that the image of trinity in the mind with its habits of love and knowledge is also insufficient. Both are insufficient because they do not provide an express image. In the first article from the second part of distinction three, however, Bonaventure queries the trinity found in the powers of the soul, namely memory, intellect and will; and never directly states whether or not these can provide a proof for the existence of trinity of persons in God, though that is the tenor of the whole surrounding discussion. He ends, instead, by agreeing that the soul's powers do not make up the same essence as the soul. This is taken to be Bonaventure's disclaimer of a rational proof in this third try, too, even though he does not say so and, in fact, hedges considerably in his supposedly destructive conclusion.

Demonstrated Features of the Exemplar

So far I have suggested what status the exemplifying features in images have, and what sort of process any demonstrative exemplification must be. The final component of this relational dynamic has just been hinted at: that the divine trinity to be proven must be the one found in orthodox creeds, which Bonaventure identified as the unity of divine essence with the trinity of divine persons. The details of this orthodoxy make up the remainder of the first book of the commentary, on how to use language so that it does not distort those claims. Yet Bonaventure's discussion of the rational evidence for trinity does not rely on that detailing, but precedes it, relying on no more than the unity of essence with trinity of persons.

Distinction I: Using and Enjoying

Giving context to this third distinction, Bonaventure begins his book by asking what is to be delighted in, what used, and what both. The answers are God and world and humans, respectively. This may be puzzling as a first distinction, other than that it is where Peter Lombard begins; until one recalls that what Bonaventure is seeking, is an expressed image, that is, expressed in knowing and loving, not merely by desiring and using it, unawares, as a matter of fact.

Distinction II: God Known by Belief

The following, second distinction is much to the point of our subject, even though it is not considered so by Bonaventure. He calls this distinction the one wherein he proceeds by authority, saving natural reason for the third distinction (div., 34B). For its quartet of questions query first whether there is only one God—note, not whether God exists; once God is known to exist, it is impossible and even unintelligible conceptually for there to be more than one. It has already been observed, however, that Bonaventure elsewhere develops the proof for the elementary undeniability of anything with the nature of God. This suggests that going on to his next questions, as to whether there are several persons, more than three or less than three, is done only by an inquirer who has already acquired satisfaction as to the existence of God, simply. It then may suggest that, when proofs of trinity are offered, it is not expected to be the proof available both to the believer and unbeliever; proof of trinity would not prove the triune existence of God, but the trinity of persons in the one God which exists. If this is the case, it would be some confirmation for what concludes his more satisfactory trinitarian proof, insofar as the soul who as image most successfully serves as a basis for proof, is one which does so because it knows God. If that is so, this would make of trinity not a theological datum, but rather a second-order philosophical one, instead of a first-order datum to be proven immediately.

Bonaventure's second question in this distinction, as to whether plurality of persons must be affirmed of God, looks to what he will address directly in the next question. His discourse is very forceful, saying in his response that not only as faith teaches, but also "all the foregoing reasons show", this must be affirmed, if one is to avoid contradiction. He then sets out another set of claims, and concludes them by saying that, once these conditions are met, then it is necessary to affirm plurality of persons in deity (38B–39A). These "foregoing reasons" all relate to the self-communicative character of God's attributes: greatest happiness (goodness, charity and joy), greatest perfection, greatest simplicity, and greatest primacy. The last two are surprising, since they could easily be seen as obstacles to trinity; but Bonaventure says that simplicity requires some nature to be in many, and not as a universal since that is as numerous as its bearers, implying that simplicity can only be in many if the many are persons each of whom bears its own simplicity. Primacy, as well, is fecund of other principles; and primacy as person is fecund of other persons. These, and the arguments from happiness and perfection, are so stated that we are "required" to draw the conclusion from them (36AB) . Similarly, the "conditions" from which one must conclude to trinity of persons are that essence is communicable, that person is naturally directed (*nata est*) upon producing another person, and that the person is ready, waiting and willing for this (38B–39A); and these conditions, he claims, are met.

It is remarkable that arguments for trinity stated with such verbal force do not for Bonaventure have the probative weight of natural reason, once the existence of God is considered to be proven by reason, and God's attributes in turn. But Bonaventure does not even query that possibility here, as he does very carefully the arguments from imagery during the next distinction, being satisfied to leave this as a datum of faith which he is only making reasonable. Similarly, while an infinity of persons is easily set aside in view of the lack of perfection in an infinity of number, the fourth and final response in this distinction two is just as forceful, in asserting that there are reasons for the necessity of the conclusion: that there are three only, no more and no less persons in God. The reasons seem not compelling, as that enjoyment needs three persons, and that the possibilities must be run through, of emanations ungenerable-unspirable, generated-unspirable, and generated-spirated (42A). He is also willing to add further reasons of "congruity", which rehearse some of those mentioned, and he is not above adding a dose of number mysticism about threeness, as well (42AB). The failure of their force, however, is one thing; the continued acceptance of them as theological matters of faith, is something else again. Yet this is what Bonaventure does, until the following distinction.

Distinction III, Part I, Sole Article: Proof of Trinity from Traces in Creatures

The first question of this third distinction, as to whether God can be known by a creature, passes lightly with the proof in his response that God is a most knowable object, as the highest light is, even to our intellect, since light completes it. This light-metaphysic is capped by his claim that the soul is somehow everything (ad 1, 49A), as will reappear later.

The feature anticipating the argument about expression which we will want to focus upon in part two, is his reply here to a fourth objection, that the infinite cannot inform the finite. He initially replies that no abstraction of God is needed, in order to inform the intellect, for God is present to the soul by truth. In addition, however, since the intellect is what knows, or is the faculty by which the person does his knowing, it must be informed by some knowledge (*notitia*). Lastly, this informing knowledge is a quasi-similitude, that is, it is not abstracted, but is impressed; and while inferior to God, it is superior to the soul (50A). Yet it does not become a similitude, because it is a change in knowledge, only. This provides suggestion of what similitude is, that sign of God which the image of God fails to adequate in the second part of this argument.

In the first part of this distinction, Bonaventure begins by affirming that God can be known, not only by a creature, but by means of creatures. To show this, he starts his methodology for proof with a statement of the causal principle, that the cause shows up in the effect. Not only is effect known from the cause, but cause is known from the effect (contra, b) . He gives the positive and the negative sides of this in regard to God: the created effects lead more to God, than they do even to other creatures; but they do so deficiently, since the highest light cannot be known by a "quasi-material" intellect (51A).

Bonaventure carries forward this methodology by discussing the picturing relationship, (ad 1) ; then his version of analogy (ad 3, both 51 B); and finally, the differences between proof by the shadow, trace and image. The discussions join the causal principle, to the principle that like is known by like, since everything is like God in one way or another (contra d, 51A.)

In picturing, first of all, Bonaventure turns us away from the detailed properties of something, and turns us toward what he calls the way of "ablation", in order to reach its general conditions. For a picture can be seen as a picture, and seen with no more than its own properties of line and symmetry, color and texture; and delight can be taken in those. Or, one may see the picture as an image, and recognize its pointing towards another being. All of the modes of representing God which Bonaventure will educe are of this latter, ablative sort.

The picture and the pictured, however, must have something common to both, some medium of knowledge. In the imaging of God by God's "picture" in soul, there can be nothing common univocally, but only analogously. (31B–32B has parallel passages on analogy for Bonaventure.) The relation (*habitudo*) of analogy can be of two sorts: either two-to-two, as a sailor and a doctor—let us presume that Bonaventure means the sailor is to his sailoring as the doctor is to her doctoring; or one-to-one, as an exemplar is to the example of it.

The representing of God seems to be all of the latter sort, given that the term 'exemplarity' is often applied to its various modes. These modes are now distinguished from each other. The shadow of God is found in all creatures, as their cause in an indeterminate sense; this leads to a knowledge only of divine persons' shared attributes, as common to all the persons. The trace of God in all things, as their triple cause—efficient, formal and final—shows God as one, true and good, common properties which are appropriated by convention to the different persons of trinity. The image of God, finally, is found only in rational beings, which can become likened (*comparator*) to God by making God an object of attention in knowledge and love as well as then in memory; this mode of demonstration shows the features of trinity which are proper to each person distinctly. No discussion of similitude is placed among these, because similitude is a distinctively grace-bound phenomenon: only one in grace has similitude, so it is not involved in this discussion of native capacities.

What we should expect to follow in the last question of this part does follow: that the answer to the question, "whether a trinity of persons with unity of essence can be known naturally through creatures," is "no", when one means by this all creatures, and not solely rational ones with their distinctive image (55A). The reason, is that plurality of supposits with unity of essence is never found among creatures.

But this we knew; the point was to find an analogous image to it, for knowing the unknown from the known is the very point of reasoning by analogy. Trinity seems immune to the threefold way traditionally used with divine analogy; for Bonaventure says our claims here must be one or the other, affirmation or denial, and we already know that to make claims even about divine simplicity cannot be done by only one or the other way alone. Bonaventure is surprisingly forceful in his denial of a natural proof by shadows and traces: such likeness never knew trinity of persons, or even plurality, in godhead. The most they could get at was a distinction among the essential properties of God (*proprietatum*), to which correspond a trinity of such appropriated attributes (*appropriate*) to particular persons, as unity, truth and goodness, but not a trinity of attributes proper (*propria*) to particular persons of trinity (55B).

Bonaventure concludes the article by reaffirming, however, that what philosophers do grasp, they hold securely. Since the stopping point (*status*) in causes which is presupposed in all philosophy is existentially grounded, in the impossibility of there being something produced from nothing if there is no still point (dub. 1; 56A), then philosophers' arguments for the existence of God are not merely persuasions by signs, but are arguments from necessity (dub. 2; 56B).

A remnant is left here, however, for the proof of trinity to be recommenced in the next part of this distinction. These denials were all made only about traces, not images (ad 3, 55B). Beyond these, there is still some way in which what is believed has likeness (*quod creditur simile*) in creatures, although not by a complete (*omnino*) likeness (resp., 55A). This is image; it resides only in what we might call subjectivity or, he, soul. Understanding the soul as to what it is, belongs to reason; but knowing it insofar as it is an image, is said by Bonaventure to belong to faith alone (ad 4, 55B). This is the claim now to be tested in the second part of the distinction.

Distinction III, Part II, Article I: Proof of Trinity from its Images in Memory, Intelligence and Will

Trinity of Substantial Powers

Bonaventure's primary way of assigning an image of God is through memory, intelligence and will. Recall that memory in Augustine, from whom this image is explicitly derived, stands for mind as a power in its most comprehensive sense, fully reflexive, upon itself, upon its own negation (forgetfulness), and upon more than what itself is within it (innate species). Bonaventure shows that an image is found in the powers, by comparison to the plurality of their acts, while the powers retain their essential unity. The acts of these powers show the distinction of one power from the other, because of the peculiar way each act of soul is disposed by its preceding act: retention of species (in memory) disposes to knowing, and knowing to loving (resp. 59B). What is spoken of as these three are powers each of which is wholly identified with itself, because reflexive: remembering is the whole memory, knowing intellectually is the whole intellect, and so of the will as well, once it is taken comprehensively as both willing and willing-not (*velle, nolle*), not simply the former (ad 6, 6OB; con. 6, 59A).

The more developed features of an image are supplied in examining these intellectual powers. The imaging faculty's conformity must be expressed. It is a perfect capacity, fully capable of God; the only faculties of this sort are those which are self-reflexive (vid. A, b, 58D). Next, it represents with distinctness the order and the origin of what is imaged. These suppositions Bonaventure accepts, despite rebutting the other points in the objection where they appear. Further on, the relation of image to the elusive similitude it fails to be is clarified a little more: image is not gratuitous, but natural, and is found in our powers as described; but similitude is gratuitous, and so it is attained only by the exercise of those powers in appropriating the similitude (ad 5, 60A). Nonetheless, image is found only in those capable (*nata*) of receiving the "image of reformation", or a similitude (con. 4, 59A), namely, intellectual agents

These data on the character of image are supplemented in Bonaventure's most lengthy response (61B) to the next question in this latter part of the distinction, whether the image is found to belong to these powers in comparison to God. The image requires: again, an express conformity to the imaged; next, that what conforms to the image, is thus conformed to the imaged (as he who sees Peter's image, sees Peter, as well) ; and so, thirdly, that the soul by having these powers of memory, intelligence and will, is made conformed to the things which it turns them upon. "When soul is turned to God, it is conformed to itself; and the image is found according to that conformity", Bonaventure says. This schema introduces a third facet of transitivity, the conformity to the imaged of what is conformed to the image.

This implies that the image of God in the powers of soul, once they are put into act, is paramount and expressed when God is their object. It is less so, secondly, when they make themselves their object; but the image is not altogether lost if those powers are ones which have had God as their object, since they are now not only conformed to God, but precisely as powers are both their own object and so also now are expressly conformed to God. Differently stated, self-reflection seems likely to bear the features of an image, although it does so only on condition of those reflective powers being directed upon the God continually present to them in their being, and formerly present to them formally as their object. Thirdly, these powers when directed upon other things, lose the express conformity to God, thereby lose their imagery, and become merely traces of God's trinity of persons (also: ad 1–3, 62A).

Notice that Bonaventure recognizes that his claims are being made in the order of knowing, not of being (ad 5, 62B): equality in the image need be among the three facets of the image, not between the image and the imaged; thus soul turns its powers to itself more because of its consubstantiality and equality to them, while it turns them toward God because of greater conformity and attractiveness (*venustatis*).

Two startling features emerge from this data. First, the object upon which the agent needs to be directed is God, in order for her faculties to image Trinity to her, not upon Trinity. For this is the object known and loved; that is the object which bears the triune feature. Such an argument allows the trinity of soul's powers to have as what they image the triune God, and to have the relationship we see they have to each other become seen also as expressing the relation of divine persons. The distinctions in God can only be distinctions of personhood, if they are not to be distinctions of nature on the one hand, or merely accidental on the other. Thus the argument keeps from becoming circular, or at least theological, such that soul's powers must already have for their object God as triune, before their relationship can be argued to be an image proving that triunity.

To repeat, the dynamic of the proof is the following. The soul knows God. It knows that it is knowing God. That is, it knows that it is conformed to God, both formally in knowledge and existentially in being. Soul knows also that it has three essential powers. It knows its three powers are conformed to God. It knows God, then, as triune in personhood.

This explains why these powers provide to soul an image of Trinity only when knowing God or the soul itself but not other creatures. The image of Trinity must be expressed, or explicit. The image of Trinity is expressed even when the knowledge of God is recognized, not only when the knowledge of Trinity is recognized. There still remains room for the discovery of Trinity in this knowledge of God, rather than the knowledge of Trinity having to precede the argument for Trinity, in a circular way.

The second corollary is a further extension of the extended rational access to this argument given earlier by Bonaventure's claim that humans in every state, not only in the state of perfection, can know God through creatures, even if less clearly (d.3, p.1, a.1, q. 3, 53B). Now Bonaventure goes on to say that sinners, too, have the image of God, because that image is present not by reason of any actual turning toward God to make God the object of our soul's powers, but by reason of their possibility of so turning (ad 4, 62A). This distances the proof Bonaventure is giving even further from having a theological character, since it no longer depends upon the fact of salvation having occurred for the thinker, but depends only upon his or her capacity for it, by nature. Granted, Bonaventure has supplied a response to this, that while 'image' refers either to the impression of a set of powers upon our nature, or to the expression coming from their use, only the exercise provides an access by imaging, not the power alone to do so. But here, when Bonaventure makes the reply just cited, he is talking only about that excercise. As well, the pilgrim of question three is always a sinner; yet he or she can know God, and so can carry out the expression of the triune image.

The capacity to conform one's intellectual apprehensions to the Trinity is not similar to the capacity to walk, when used as descriptions of human beings. Both capacities may be affirmed, even when one cannot exercise them. But while walking may wait upon sight of some walker ever to be affirmed, the grasp of Trinity occurs where one knows of God and knows of soul, even if in resistance to that awareness.

Unity of Substance

What is it then, which keeps Bonaventure from concluding "yes" to the question with which he concluded the first part of this distinction: can triunity be naturally known from creatures? It appears to be because, in his final question of this article, whether the soul's three powers have the same essence as the soul does (or, more accurately, are the same in essence with it (*idem in essentia cum anima*), there lies the other part of triunity: not only three equal divine persons; but also one divine nature. If the agent's powers are an image only to the extent of leading to the first, but not the second, they cannot lead necessarily to knowledge of the triune God. To this question Bonaventure answers "no". But he withdraws from a simple negation, by distinguishing his answer. Soul's powers are not the same essence as soul is, in the most thoroughgoing way this can be said; but it is truly said in a derivative sense (64B).

His two ways of getting at this, in terms of the several senses of 'nature' and of 'essence', will be seen; but first the obvious sense in which the answer must be no should be glimpsed, from his answer to objections. There, in reply to a query based on Aristotle's texts, Bonaventure replies (ad 4, 65A) that if the soul and its powers were simply the same, then it would be the same event to be existing and to be acting, and the agent would always be acting, then, since she is always existing. That the principles of being and of acting are the same, is true only of the remote principle: form is the immediate and proximate principle of being; but it is only the mediate and remote principle for acting. The immediate and proximate principle for acting is potency, or in terms more appropriate to this context, is the powers, the faculties of soul.

To this explanation in terms of form, Bonaventure adds two more, first in terms of nature, and then of essence. Something's powers are said to be 'natural' to it, or of the same genus as it is, in two ways, firstly (d. 3, p. 2, a. 2, resp, 64AB). Either the powers have a natural mode of existence in it, or a mode of existence which goes out from it naturally. The first is the way a boxer or runner has the power whereby he boxes or runs easily. The second is of two sorts, as it goes out from an agent either with some accident, or else immediately. An example of the first is that, from fire, comes the power of heating along with the fire's heat. An example of the other is that, from the parent, comes the power of generating by inducing the final form. This last sort of power is not of some other genus than is the substance, and is described by being reduced back to the genus to which the substance belongs, as a sort of substantial difference.

Memory, intelligence and will are of this last sort. They contrast with, for example, an attribute of cleverness, or again a skill at making sound arguments, once a person knows how to do that, which are qualities in one or the other of the first two ways Bonaventure distinguished. The three imaging powers, instead, emerge from the soul, as from their substance and their subject; and they do so immediately. This is because the soul is a spiritual substance, which is present to itself and always one with itself; and so its powers are ones for recall of itself, knowing itself, and loving itself. These three powers, therefore, are consubstantial to soul, and are the same genus as it is, by returning back to it. Not totally the same in essence, nor totally differing as belonging to a different genus, these three powers of soul are the same by any way of "reduction".

One further approach Bonaventure makes is by the notion of essence. 'Essential' is said primarily of a thing's genus-and-species totality; it is said, next, of its matter-and-form constitution; and then, of its metaphysical principles, without which it can neither be nor be known, such as the transcendentals of unity, truth and goodness. The weakest sense of all for 'essential' is that without which something could not be thought to have its being in the appropriate manner; these are the powers of soul, and they are what constitute the image—the least consubstantial with or essential to the soul, the agent.

But they are still not of another genus. While this explanation of essence is preferred only to make the explanation by the Fathers acceptable, it does agree with his own, in terms of nature, already considered.

The terms are given some explanation in Bonaventure's example of someone's appearance: Martin's appearance, presuming that *similitudo* is not being used here in its technical sense (resp., 64B). Martin's likeness is not Martin: it has not such an identity that they are one in number. But, secondly (though Bonaventure did not complete this half of his example), Martin's likeness is not (of) something different from Martin: it has not such a diversity that they differ in genus, differing through and through (*penitus*). Thirdly, the way in which it is of the same genus is by reduction: it "goes out", and so it differs; but it does not pass to another genus. Thus it remains a likeness, and not a directedness (*intentionis*), as it would be if it left the subject and did not return, like radiance from a light-source.

This is not clear; but it can perhaps be made somewhat more so by bringing to bear Bonaventure's earlier use of the Aristotelean classification of sciences upon Peter Lombard, to show that his method is investigative, while still scriptural (proem., q. 2, ad 4, 10A). Not every determination which draws off one part of a study makes for a subalternated science, but only one which "draws it away" in a special manner, i.e., by reference to different principles. Thus the science subalternated to geometry is not the science of the straight line, but is rather, e.g., the science of visual lines. And the Lombard's work is a subalternate of scriptural studies, since it treats matters intelligible by reason, not those believable by authority, although it returns to the certainty of the latter when its own fails. An activity "goes out" from an agent, then, when additional genera of principles are employed, but not so far as to deprive the activity of its certain foundations in the nature of the agent. So these powers of soul can be reduced back to the essence of soul, because their different principles of being do not separate them from soul as their foundation.

This explanation was extended, in what preceded, in order to have seen whether there is any reason to empty the import from Bonaventure's admission that the powers of soul are the same in essence as it is, even if only by reduction. There is no reason to diminish it. The image of God in these powers of the soul is, then, not only trinitarian as he had acknowledged just before this, but is also unitarian, which he had seemed to doubt. Nothing is missing for Bonaventure to have answered "yes", to the question he refrained from asking here, the question he did ask and answered no, at the end of the preceding question, and again in the last article of this distinction: "whether trinity of persons with unity of essence can be known naturally through creatures?"

Distinction III, Part II, Article II: Proof of Trinity from its Image in Mind, Knowledge and Love

The final article of this distinction is a denouement after what just preceded. This final trinity of mind, knowledge and love promises more, not because it includes the substance of soul along with its habits, as it does (and I have argued that Bonaventure admitted that the preceding trinity did that), but because there is reflexivity of the habits when in act upon themselves, making possible the order, the equality and the consubstantiality needed for the interaction among divine persons (q. 2, 69AB). Yet from the first response we are told that this image is not proper, but secondary; and that the preceding image of trinity was more proper and fitted to trinity than this is (q. 1, 67A). Here we have the unique substance of soul which Bonaventure said he found lacking in the preceding article; but only two properties of the substance appear, not three. And this expectation of inadequacy is confirmed in Bonaventure's "no" to the final question, whether this image necessarily leads to knowledge of three divine persons as such. Attributing its trinity of features to God allows us only to attribute to

God a trinity of attributed properties (*appropriate*) which all the philosophers knew, and so which was all the philosophers could know—rather than the essential properties of God (*propria*), namely, the three divine persons in unity of essence. Only faith sufficed to give a perfect knowledge of this image, although once faith has done so, the image can then do the job, even if no job remains to be done. Bonaventure repeats his earlier observations about pictures: knowing this image as image will lead necessarily to triune God, but knowing it simply for the features it has, without any further "ablation", will not; and knowing it in the former way depends upon faith (q. 3, resp. , 70A) . The theological virtues of faith, hope and charity stand in, thereafter, for its elements, which become reflexive not only upon themselves but upon their imaging selves, what he concludes to be the higher level image, the similitude (*imagine similitudinis*; q. 1, 67A).

CONCLUSION

While Bonaventure's conclusions as to the first and third of these images are sound, this study has shown that the image of trinity by memory, intelligence and will provides adequate grounds for and leaves sufficient room for the conclusion, that Bonaventure provides at least one proof for the existence of triune God based on natural reason alone.

REFERENCES

Aertsen, Jan A. 'Filosofia cristiana: ¿primacia del ser "versus" primacia del bien?' *Anuario filosofico* 33 (2000) 339–361.

Alston, William P. 'Swinburne and Christian Theology', *International Journal for Philosophy of Religion* 41 (1997) 35–57.

Barbone, Steven. 'St. Bonaventure's Journey *into* God', *Franciscanum* 37 (1996) 57–65.

Bartel, Timothy. 'The Plight of the Relative Trinitarian', *Religious Studies* 24 (1988) 129–155.

Beuchot, Mauricio. 'Significado y cara'cter general de la pruebas de Dios en el pensamiento bonaverilriano', *Revista de filosofia* (Mexico) 20 (1987) 304–317.

Bowman, Leonard J. 'Bonaventure, Hierarchy and Perennialism', *Contemporary Philosophy* 13 (1991) 10–15.

Bracken, Joseph A. *Society and Spirit: A Trinitarian Cosmology*. Selinsgrove PA: Susquehanna University Press, 1991.

Charron, William, and John P. Doyle. 'On the Self-Refuting Statement "There Is No Truth": A Medieval Treatment', *Vivarium* 31 (1993) 241–266.

Clark, Mary T. 'An Inquiry Into Personhood', *Review of Metaphysics* 46 (1992) 3–28.

———. 'Augustine's Theology of the Trinity: Its Relevance', *Dionysius* 13 (1989) 71–84.

Cousins, Ewert H. 'Fecundity and the Trinity; An Appendix to Chapter Three of *The Great Chain of Being*', in *Jacob's Ladder and the Tree of Life; Concepts of Hierarchy and the Great Chain of Being*, ed. Marion Leather Kuntz, Paul G. Kuntz. New York: Lang, 1987. Pp. 73-82.

Darcus, Roy. 'The Third Theorem: Contemporary Expression of Trinitarian Thought', *Dionysius* 11 (1987) 147–180.

De Boni, Luis Alberto. 'A Escola Franciscana: de Boaventura a Ockham', *Veritas* 45 (2000) 317–338.

Dewan, Lawrence, 'St. Thomas, St. Bonaventure, and the Need to Prove the Existence of God', in *Philosophy and Culture*, V, 3, ed. Venant Cauchy, 841–844. Montreal: Editions Montmorency, 1988.

Emery, Gilles. 'Essentialism or Personalism in the Treatise on God in Saint Thomas Aquinas', *Thomist* 64 (2000)521–563.

———. 'Le traité de saint Thomas sur la Trinité dans la Somme contre les Gentils', *Revue thomiste* 96 (1996) 5–40.

Fedoryka, Kateryna. 'Certitude and the Contuition: St. Bonaventure's Contribution to the Theory of Knowledge', *Aletheia* 6 (1994) 163–197.

Feser, E. 'Has Trinitarianism Been Shown To Be Coherent?' *Faith and Philosophy* 14 (1997) 87–97.

Feser, Edward C. 'Swinburne's Tritheism', *International Journal for Philosophy of Religion* 42 (1997) 175–184.

Fischer, Konrad. 'Hinweise zur Gotteslehre Bonaventuras', in *San Bonaventura Maestro di vita francescana e di sapienza cristiana*, ed. A. Pompei. Roma: Pontificia Faculta Teologica San Bonaventura, 1976. Val. I, pp. 513–525.

Forrest, Peter. 'Divine Fission: A New Way of Moderating Social Trinitarianism', *Religious Studies* 34 (1998) 281–297.

Hankey, Wayne J. 'Dionysius Becomes An Augustinian. Bonaventure's Itinerarium vi', in *Studia Patristica* 29 (Leuven: Peeters, 1997) 252–259.

——— 'Theoria Versus Poesis: Neoplatonism and Trinitarian Difference in Aquinas, John Milbank, Jean-Luc Marion and John Ziziolas', *Modern Theology* 15 (1999) 387–415.

Hedley, Douglas. 'Pantheism, Trinitarian Theism and the Idea of Unity: Reflections on the Christian Concept of God', *Religious Studies* 32 (1996) 61–77.

Hellman, J. A. Wayne. *Ordo; Untersuchung eines Grundgedanken in derTheologie Bonaventuras*. Muenchen: F. Schoeningh, 1974.

Henningfeld, Jochem. 'Verbum-Signum: Le definition du langage chez s. Augustin et Nicolas de Cues', *Archives de philosophie* (1991) 255–268.

Hill, William J. 'The Doctrine of God After Vatican II', *Thomist* 51 (1987) 395–4.

——— 'Rescuing Theism: A Bridge Between Aquinas and Heidegger', *Heythrop Journal* 27 (1986) 377–393.

Keane, Kevin P. 'Ordo Bonitatis: The Summa Fratris Alexandri and Lovejoy's Dilemma', in *Jacob's Ladder and the Tree of Life. Concepts of Hierarchy and The Great Chain of Being*, ed. Marion Leather Kuntz, Paul G. Kuntz. New York: Lang, 1987. Pp. 55–72.

Kern, Iso. 'Trinity. Theological Reflections of a Phenomenologist', in *Essays in Phenomenology*, ed. Steven W. Laycock, James G. Hart. Albany: SUNY Press, 1986. Pp. 23–37.

Kretzmann, Norman. 'Reason in Mystery', *Philosophy* 25 (1988) 15–39, Suppl.1989 (*The Philosophy in Christianity*, ed. Geoffrey Vesey. The Royal Institute of Philosophy Lecture Series, No.25).

Kuntz, Paul G. 'The Hierarchical Vision of St. Bonaventure', in *Jacob's Ladder and the Tree of Life; Concepts of Hierarchy and The Great Chain of Being*, ed. Marion Leather Kuntz, Paul G. Kuntz. New York: Lang, 1987. Pp. 83–100.

La Cugna, Catherine Mowry. 'Philosophers and Theologians on the Trinity', *Modern Theology* 2 (1986) 169–181.

Lancaster, Sarah H. 'Three-Personed Substance: The Relational Essence of the Triune God in Augustine's De Trinitate', *Thomist* 60 (1996) 123–139.

Langston, Douglas. 'The Spark of Conscience: Bonaventure's View of Conscience and Synderesis', *Franciscan Studies* 53 (1993) 79–95.

Lash, Nicholas. 'Considering the Trinity', *Modern Theology* 2 (1986) 183–196.

Layman, Stephen C. 'Tritheism and the Trinity', *Faith and Philosophy* 5 (1988) 291–298.

Leinsle, Ulrich G. *Res et Signum; Das Verstandnis Zeichenhafter in der Theologie Bonaventuras*. Muenchen: F. Schoeningh, 1976.

Mackey, Louis. 'Redemptive Subversions: The Christian Discourse of St. Bonaventure', in *The Autonomy of Religious Belief*, ed. Frederick J. Crosson. Notre Dame: University of Notre Dame Press, 1981. Pp. 38–59.

——— 'Singular and Universal: A Franciscan Perspective', *Franciscan Studies* 39 (1979, publ. 1982) 130–164.

Martinich, A. P. 'God, Emperor and Relative Identity', *Franciscan Studies* 39 (1979) 180–191.

Milbank, John. 'The Second Difference: For A Trinitarianism Without Reserve', *Modern Theology* 2 (1986) 213–234.

O'Donnell, John J. 'The Doctrine of Trinity in Recent German Theology', *Heythrop Journal* 23 (1982) 153–167.

Pieretti, Antonio. 'L'Itinerarium di S. Bonaventura come ermeneutica ontologica' *Rivista di filosofia neo-scolastica* 79 (1987) 313–320.

Plantigna, Cornelius, Jr. 'Gregory of Nyssa and the Social Analogy of the Trinity,' *Thomist* 50 (1986) 325–352.

Purcell, Michael. 'Leashing God with Levinas: Tracing a Trinity with Levinas', *Heythrop Journal* 40 (1999) 301–318.

Reichberg, Gregory. "The Communication of the Divine Nature: Thomas's Response to Neoplatonism,' *Proceedings of the American Catholic Philosophical Association* 66 (1992) 215–228.

Rezende, Vanio Terezinha de. 'A imagem humana da trindade em Agostinho', *Educacao e Filosofia* 15 (2001) 259–276.

Rudebusch, George. 'Aristotelean Predication, Augustine and the Trinity', *Thomist* 53 (1989) 587–597.

Russo, Renato. *La metodologia del savere nel sermone di San Bonaventura 'Unus est deus magister voster Christus'*. Grattaferrata: Ed. Collegii S. Bonaventura, 1982.

Sanders, Theresa. 'A Postmodern Trinity?' *in The 1994 Annual of Hermeneutics and Social Concern*, ed. Justus George Lawler. New York: Continuum, 1994.

Scala, Albina Aurora. 'Il passaggio dal credibile all'intelligibile nel *Commento alle Sentenze* di san Bonaventura', in *San Bonaventura Maestro di vita francescana e di sapienza cristiana*, ed. A. Pompei. Roma: Pontificia Faculta Teologica San Bonaventura, 1976. Vol. 1, pp. 553–562.

Scapin, Pietro. ' "Dio da Dio". Approccio bonaventuriano del problema di Dio', in *Teologia e Filosofia nel Pensiero di S. Bonaventura; Contributi per una nuova interpretazione*, n.ed. Brescia: Morcelliana, 1974. Pp. 139–176.

Seifert, Josef. '"Si Deus est Deus, Deus est": Reflections on St. Bonaventure Interpretation of St. Anselm's Ontological Argument', *Franciscan Studies* 52 (1992) 215–231.

Vezzosi, Giovanni. 'Sulla relazione in San Tomasso: In dialogo con Krempel', *Sapienza* 54 (2001) 489–496.
Viladesau, Richard. 'The Trinity in Universal Revelation', *Philosophy and Theology* 4 (1990) 317–334.
Wagner, Raynald. 'Zum Gottesbegriff bei Bonaventura; Parmenides und Bonaventura' in *Bonaventura: Studien zu seiner Wirkungsgeschichte*, n. ed. Werl: Dietrich–Coelde, 1976. Pp. 33–40.
Williams, Rowan. 'Trinity and Revelation', *Modern Theology* 2 (1986) 197–212.
Zabzebski, Linda. 'Christian Monotheism', *Faith and Philosophy* 6 (1989) 3–18.

NOTES

1. All references in my text are to the parts, pages and columns of his *Commentarium in libris IV sententiarum Magistri Petri Lombardis* as found in the *Doctoris serafici S. Bonaventurae opera theologica selecta* (ad Claras Aquas, Florentiae, 1938). This text is found at pages 66–96, of the 1886 Quarrachi critical edition of his *Omnia Opera*, volume I. Joseph A. Buijs and Lawrence Dewan, O.P., are thanked for their correction of some of the deficiencies in this study.

2. John F. Wippel, Allan B. Wolter, *Medieval Philosophy: From St. Augustine to Nicholas of Cusa* (New York: Free Press, 1969).

3. References within the text to current literature are to writings in *References*.

CHAPTER EIGHT

CIVIL OBLIGATION IN BONAVENTURE AND 20TH CENTURY ANARCHISTS

The place to start with a friar is with his Rule. That is Bonaventure's final word to distinction 44 in his second book of his Commentary on the Sentences.[1].

> [A friar] does not bind himself to do all that he will be told to do, but to do what is expressed in his Rule. ... So he is not bound to obey in everything.... Thus there are limits placed on his promise of obedience. ... Friars are not simply ordered to obey their superirors in everything, but "in everything that they have promised the Lord to observe and that is not contrary to their soul and Rule" (chap. 10)

His first word there concerns sin and coercion, his second concerns coercion and obedience, and his last concerns obedience and religious vow. This chapter concerns the second word, Bonaventure's study of civil obligation, but sin and especially vows have to be used to interpret that duty.

Bonaventure implies there is no obligation to obey the law earlier in his commentary. As will be seen below, contenporaary political philosophers Joseph Raz and John Simmons seem to make a similar claim to Bonaventure. While Bonaventure is reluctant to lay this obligation upon humans in our original nature, the discourse of our contemporaries has little to do with nature, fallen or otherwise.

Raz says : "I shall argue that there is no obligation to obey the law even in a good society whose legal system is just."[2] Again, he writes, "Consent to political authority, where given, is often free. It does not follow that it is binding. ... Where it is binding, it cannot be used as a way of endowing anyone with authority where that person had none."[3] He clarifies elsewhere, "My basic position is not that no one has any moral reason ever to take account of the existence of the law. I argue that the extent of the obligation to obey varies from person to person. In no case is the moral obligation as extensive as the legal obligation."[4]

Simmons writes, "According to philosophical anarchism, few, if any, citizens in existing political societies have political obligations, and existing governments lack the correletive right to command."[5] Again, he argues, "States may not demand that we obey their laws; but they may legitimately punish us for doing what is in fact contrary to law, when our so acting also breaches a moral duty."[6] Finally, he writes that "[p]hilosophical anarchists maintain that we (or most of us) have no political obligations, that all arguments purporting to extablish general political obligations fail, perhaps even necessarily fail, as a result of a necessary clash between state authority and the autonomy required for individual obligation)."[7]

Bonaventure's reluctance to lay down an obligation to obey the law is surprising since throughout his later writing he expresses order and obligation abundantly. His colloquia, sermons and treatises expound a metaphysics rooted in threefold order, drawn by inclination toward its goal, and hierarchical in its social setting. Inequality, subordination and authority characterize it. As there is hierarchy in Trinity, among angels, within creation, the soul and the Church, so there is hierarchy in the ecclesiastical and lay orders, still conceived organically. The justice of this hierarchy involves guidelines for living together and for ruling. All the conditions for an obligation to obey law seem to be present. This is Matthew DeBenedictis' characterization.[8]

In contrast to these later developments, our sentential commentator approves the second disjunct of the question (II Sent., dist. 44, art. 2, qu. 1), "is the power for governing in man as a natural institution, or as a punishment for fault". He distinguishes different senses of power and different senses of nature in order to do this. Power is of three sorts, one kind for managing the use of things, another for giving rational direction, and a third which involves coercing subjects. Bonaventure understands the term "power" in the question's title with reference only to the third type of power.[9]

Human nature also has three senses, as original, as fallen, and in glory. Bonaventure refers only to nature in the present condition, that of fallen nature, in order to answer the question. His answer, then, is that in our present condition the power for coercing subjects is natural, but that it is unnatural to our original nature.[10] The power for coercing subjects is a punishment for original sin, and is needed so as to bring order among the humans who find themselves in that condition.

Michael Malloy does not bear in mind Bonaventure's teaching on sin and vow when he asserts that Bonaventure gives little rationale for civil obligation in his teaching on natural law.[11] Molloy glances at the power to sin in article one, but overlooks the subjection to governing power among Christians and religious in the third article. His focus is on the power of governing in the second article. There he interprets Bonaventure as sliding away from a firm assertion that human nature welcomes civil authority in its every condition—in innocence, in fall, and in glory. Malloy finds Bonaventure giving no role for authoritative power except to control and to punish sin.

Interpreted as he is by Malloy, our saint is fellow traveller to contemporary anarchists. Both deny a natural duty to obey the law. But while Bonaventure affirms primarily the strong, traditional (Augustinian) *non-natural* duty to obey the law, according to Malloy, such anarchist writers as Simmons, Green and Raz affirm many other *natural* duties for obeying the law, such as mutual protection, the maintenance of just institutions, and achieving the civil virtue upon which the coordination needed for compliance is based. These duties provide moral reasons to act in law-abiding ways; but they are reasons for those actions, not for the law-abiding.

What the contemporary anarchist denies is a duty to obey the law simply because it has been made law. That law does bind in this way roots itself in Lockean consent theory which is the dominant modern theory of political obligation from Hobbes to Rawls, perhaps stretched back even to the conciliarist theory that rises immediately after Bonaventure. The contrary notion that law does not bind in this way stems from the anarchists' denial that consent—actual or hypothetical, explicit or implicit—occurs when citizens receive and accept public benefits. If there were a civic obligation to the law per se arising from the acceptance of societal goods, citizens would have to consent; but since citizens do not consent, civic obligation to the law does not arise.

The issues which have to be treated in order to clarify this topic are these: First, how correct is Malloy interpreting Bonaventure on this question? Then, does Bonaventure's position presage either the modern consensualist position or the contemporary anarchist position?

Bonaventure certainly appears to give Malloy good grounds for his claim in the core passages of distinction 44. What Molloy does not attend to, however, is Bonaventure's gratuitous limitation of civil power to this third kind, to dominion[12]. Molloy also accepts unqualifiedly Bonaventure's claim that civil power is a stricture upon freedom, as though authority in the other two senses were not limiting, too. Moreover, this stricture is equivalent to slavery (II Sent., dist. 44, art.2, qu. 1, resp.,para 1), not merely to the give and take of living together.[13]

What makes the discussion go awry on these points is the context for their consideration. Despite the medievals' genius for turning rigid procedural confines into occasions for novelty, this entire discussion is confined to the questions posed by Peter Lombard. Lombard questions first the potential (*potentia*) for sin, introducing an opinion that holds that only the power to do good is from God, not the power to do evil and hence neither is the defect of sin from God.[14] The positive *potentia* seems to mean will and knowledge, but Lombard says these are only a metaphor for the power; in fact, *potentia* is not defined further. Lombard does not distinguish *potentia* as the metaphysical principle (will and knowledge) coordinate with act (*actus*), from *potentia* as the narrow capacity for action (*actio*), the defective performance.

But Lombard then seems to subscribe to an opinion that blends both these senses, which are matters of fact, into a third (suddenly normative) sense, called *potestas*: power for evil comes from God, from whom all power comes. *Potentia* for evil now is *potestas* for evil, and that *potestas* over evil explicitly means authority, secular authority. From there on, the problem is insoluble without changing the terms: human nature is evil only as fallen; so power for evil also belongs only to our fallen state, whether as the individual's capability, as the individual's defect, or as the society's law. Lombard cannot separate law from sin, once he has defined power that way.

Nor can Bonaventure, starting from Lombard, until his later writing. This is why Bonaventure in distinction 44 can link civil authority only to domination and not to rational direction; to restriction and not to freedom; and to slavery and not to citizenship. Lombard's confusion on this point is not something Bonaventure challenges in his *dubia* about the Master. In fact, the moment where Lombard makes his error, marked by his shift from *potentia* to *potestas* while adding to *potestas* the meaning of *potentia*, is lost in Bonaventure by his use of both terms throughout the entire discussion. He uses also *praesidendum* and *praelatio* alongside *dominandum* and *dominium* throughout the distinction; so no systematic terminological distinction is available.[15]

From that unpromising starting point, it is remarkable that Bonaventure or any other Sentences commentator could extricate natural authority as far as they did. Bonaventure's escape could have come from his technique of differentiating the two other senses of power or authority, namely power or authority to realize one's will, and power or authority to give reasonable direction, instrumental and sapiential reason, respectively. Malloy is right, however, that Bonaventure failed to invoke those available senses for his appreciation of legal authority here; and the reason why is purely contextual.[16]

Bonaventure's standpoint for achieving this result is, however, equivalent to that of the contemporary anarchists, for whom the question also is whether there is an obligation to obey the law not when it is unjust, but even in a just regime. This is what Bonaventure, too, is considering in this commentary, while making ample room in his later writing for refusal of obedience when the regime is unjust.

Anarchical rejection of a general obligation to obey the law begins with a paradox of authority and autonomy. The paradox lies in realizing that moral obligations to act as the law requires actually undermine legal obligation, instead of supporting it. Within a just state there are many moral obligations whose content the law duplicates. Forbidding harm to others is the clear example. But a person who avoids harming will take it as an insult that the reason he does so is because the law obliges him to avoid it. He already has a reason, and the law is superfluous. Surely, some persons need the force of law to motivate their restraint, but then the obligation of law is theirs alone. No general obligation to obey the law follows.

The same is true generally for coordination problems. Many necessary social outcomes can only be produced by coordinated effort, and this effort is accomplished by the law. Only if the law places a uniform obligation upon everyone will the "free riders" on these schemes of social benefit not dissuade everyone else from cooperating. But this equally utilitarian reason for cooperating is true only in those cases where it is true. If one can avoid the performance without impeding the outcome, he has not brought himself under the obligation. Again, no general obligation to obey the law follows.

Of course, there is a tautological legal obligation to obey the law. Seldom is it stated in the law; but any legal dictum implies that it is itself legal, meaning that there is a legal obligation to obey it, when obedience is what it requires. The consequence is that, if apprehended in contravention, the legal punishment may be incurred. This, however, has little to do with whether this person is liable for failure to carry out a moral obligation to that same performance.

While definitionally anyone who identifies himself with the legal regime of obligations is morally liable for their performance, not everyone within the jurisdiction of a given regime identifies himself in this way. Some of those who do that explicitly, do that under public coercion as a condition for avoiding public detriments, and so the consensual nature of their performance is spoiled, and with it the obligation.

Once utilitarian considerations become the basis of paarticular patterns of obedience, not only do we not have the wherewithal to generate a general obligation to obey the law, the primary work of contemporary anarchists is readied. But the deontology of a general obligation to obey the law remains to be considered; persons who receive public benefits are, in fairness, obliged to return public burdens, in particular, that of obeying the law of the regime.

The anarchists' reply is that, while true that consent to benefits establishes obligation as much as direct consent to the obligation does, nonetheless few in contemporary societies give that consent. Benefits that some can do without (occupational safety) can be imposed without asking; even benefits which some oppose (national defence, by pacifists) are forced upon the citizen. As well, benefits which cannot be done without (police, safe foods, postal services) are forced upon one by delivery systems which some would refuse. Any receipt of benefits which imposes an obligation reciprocal to the burden of obedience, must be active and not passive, must be at least as consensual as barely accepting, before it can oblige one to make a fair response. While it seems clear that express consent or even representative consent does not involve all the persons in our societies, anarchists argue that neither does this tacit or implicit consent. When consent does occur, then consenting to benefits does ground legal obligation for those who consent. But they are not all the people, and perhaps are a diminshing few; so no legal obligation common to all the citizens is generated, which could serve as the universal counterpart to the wholistic authority of the state. Political obligation there may be, but it is spotty and scattered.

The central modern assumption is that consent can legitimate the imposition of legal burdens; the widespread contemporary reply is that consent cannot, does not, or ought not occur. While this modern assumption is not one which the high medieval theorist can make, there nonetheless are medieval analogies to it.

Bonaventure's most prominent one and the one most free of theological prejudgment is his reply that freedom is the natural state of human being (II Sent., dist. 44, art. 2, qu. 2,.sed contra.c).[17] This, he says, is a proof that civil authority cannot be natural, since it brings slavery. Bonaventure means by slavery not the metaphorical slavery of the well-off and self-directive citizen under the protection of the law, but slavery in the literal sense of unbounded subjection to the dictate of a master, good or bad. In that sense, legal order brings such a condition only to those who break the law and are punished.

But the dubious identification of the law with slavery is less important than his remarkable claim that freedom is the natural human state, that is, the freedom not to be enslaved. Freedom is lost in the fallen state, and is replaced with civil oppression as punishment for sin; but the sense of freedom that remains in the fallen state, as the freedom to act under law, even when penalites attend its failure, is close to the sense of freedom that philosophical anarchists depend upon, not to mention more traditional theorists.

In view of this we may attempt to escape the confines of the scholarly apparatus which restricts Bonaventure's sentential commentary. (1) Bonaventure there identifies alternative states of nature which have alternative sources of obligation to the present fallen state, even if he does not pursue them; on their side anarchists identify alternative sources for civic order than a general obligation to obey the law. (2) Bonaventure sees all citizens in a fallen state, which merits their servitude to authority; whereas anarchists seen some citizens as unreliable, if not fallen, and who themselves are the only ones who need to have a legal obligation imposed. (3) While Bonaventure finds no obligation to obey the law of civil society based upon our rational nature, he does find a global obligation to be subject in a state of fallen nature; anarchists find only a piecemeal obligation to obey the law, based on circumstances peculiar to a state of affairs, not a state of nature.

The presumption underlying assertion of a global obligation is that legitimate authority and legal obligation are two sides of the same normative phenomenon. If a political authority is not morally impaired, in whole or in part, for Bonaventure the legitimacy of that authority coincides with the legitimacy of its imposition of the duty to obey law. The regime is an authority in regard to all of its citizens, so its authorized law is imposed upon all, and with that an obligation to obey the law.

> So [Christians] because of the inclination to evil and the concupiscencees struggling in their members, whence arise wars and conflicts, need rule by a worldly superior just like other people—and thus they are subject to one in proportion to his power, and are obligated more or less greatly. ... So it must be acknolwledged that Christians are under obligation to their worldly rulers, although not in all things but only those which are not contrary to God, and not even in all of these but in such matters as are demanded reasonably in line with proper practice, such as taxes and rents and such like.[18]

The anarchical perspective starts from the other side, with the individual's construction or acceptance of the political authority. The authority may be received for those purposes that led to constituting it. The citizen's autonomy, however, is both the source for that constitution, and also continues to prevail beyond it. Authority and obligation are not, then, two sides of a symmetrical coin, but have each an independent relationship to their source in citizens' autonomy.

The modern presumption of the normative force to political consent may be outside the reach of a pre-conciliarist medieval. Nonetheless, the contemporary solution has some resonance in the perfection of medieval normativity: religious vows. Those vows are taken on as obligations not because their performance is commonly demanded from all, but because they are open invitations for consensual commitment. While this may be no solution in a public space which is diminishingly Christian, and vanishingly Franciscan, it does give purchase upon the contemporary anarchist's solution. The anarchist attributes the normative force to consent, but denies that consent occurs toward law. Bonaventure attributes normative force to consenting by the vow of obedience; religious are obliged to obey superiors, because they have vowed to do so, that is, because they have consented to do so.[19]

Bonaventure, moreover, in answering whether religious are obliged to obey superiors in everything, answers no: they are obliged by vow to obey only regarding what their rule requires, because that is all they have vowed. This is not the perfection of "the life of perfection", he says; but this is its obligatory reality. The normative conclusion is that even the consensually legitimated state of obligation contains no global obligation to obey, to everything the superior orders, but only those performances to which the friar has consented by vow. This is an outcome remarkably similar to the contemporary anarchists' conclusions from the commonplaces of modern political philosophy.

Developing this, if not as the sole appreciation of law, then as a supplemental resource for it, would involve drawing the following limit to the comparison. While some of what the law requires is obligatory even without the law, none of what the vow requires is obligatory apart from the vow. But such limitation does not obliterate the main point of comparison: that as vow makes obligatory what it does because of the vow, because of consent, so law purports to make obligatory what is not otherwise obligatory because that is required by law, that is, because of consent to the law. But that consent, for the contemporary anarchist, is often missing and, with it, the legal obligation.

It is clear that this resolution is important to Bonaventure by reason of his belonging to the family of St. Francis. Lombard, living nearly a hundred years before mendicant friars became theologians., did not even mention in this context the issue of whether religious are obligated to obey. Friar Thomas Aquinas, in one of the few other commentaries to use the opportunity of Lombard's question to address political obligation, also introduced here the question of religious obligation, with most of the same arguments as Bonaventure, but related it to his order's use of the Rule of St. Augustine.

Brother Bonaventure, however, explicitly relates the issue to his own rule, the Rule of St. Francis. As ever, the way to a friar is through his Rule.

One final wish to make Bonaventure's discourse yet more Franciscan, because more Christian, is that it have expanded beyond the three conditions of human nature—original, fallen, glorified—to include the fourth: human nature as redeemed. While still "groaning", release has already begun since redemption has already been won. At least some visibility must attach to this change. Lombard was too early for this perspective; Francis was the one again to celebrate it. In this perspective, authority can again impose obligations pursuant to rational direction, Bonaventure's second kind of *potentia / potestas*, but one he reserved only for original nature in his sentential commentary.

Such obligation is consistent with anarchists' piecemeal design of civil obligation, since rational direction is in play where it is needed, and not when not, rather than globally. More than that, law and legal obligation thereby regain the wherewithall to endure past even this state of human nature, and into the next. Only criminal law, the "administration of persons," withers away in the Marxian "heaven" of classless society. There is no reason to think that sensitive planning for the "administration of things", of resources, will no longer be needed in the Christian heaven of resurrected bodies, nor that there will be any less call for its Christian philosophy of law.

NOTES

1. [N]on arctat se ad faciendum omnia quae sibi fuerint imperata, sed ad faciendum ea quae in Regula expressa sunt. ... [N]on sic arctatur ad obediendum in omnibus. ... Et ideo fines ponuntur promissioni obedientiae. ... [N]on simpliciter praecipitur fratriibus suis praelatis in omnibus obedire, sed "in omnibus quae promisserunt Domino observare et non sunt contraria animae et Regulae suae" (cap. 10). Bonaventurae *Commentaria in IV libros sententiarum magistri Petri Lombardi*, in Opceia omnia (Ad Claras Aquas : Collegium S.Bonaventurae, 1882–1902; hereafter cited as Quaracchi), in *Opera theologica selecta doctoris seraphici s. Bonaventurae*, ed. Leonardo M. Bello (Firenze: Quaracchi, 1938); II Sent., dist 44, Art. 3, qu. 2, ad 6 [1014a–b].

2. Joseph Raz. *The Authority of Law; Essays on Law and Morality* (Oxford: Clarendon Press, 1979), 234..

3. Joseph Raz. *The Morality of Freedom* (Oxford: Clarendon Press, 1988), 89, 90.

4. Joseph Raz, *Ethics in the Public Domain; Essays in the Morality of Law and Politics.* (Oxford: Clarendon Press, 1994), 3311. See, for a parallel position, Leslie Green, *The Authority of the* State (Oxford : Clarendon Press, 1998), sep. Chaps. 8 and 9.

5. A. John Simmons, "The Anarchist Position: A Reply to Klosko and Senor", *Philosophy and Public Affairs* 16.3 (Sum., 1987), 269–279, ast pg. 269, restated at 275.

6. A. John Simmons, *On the Edge of Anarchy; Locke, Consent, and the Limits of Society*.(Princeton University Press, 1993), 265.

7. A. John Simmons, "Associative Political Obligations", *Ethics* 106 (1996), 247–273. For a different version of this position, see Robert Paul Wolff, *In Defence of Anarchism* (New York: Harper and Row, 1970).

8. Matthew M. DeBenedictis, *The Social Thought of Saint Bonaventure; A Study in Social Philosophy* (Washington DC: The Catholic University of America Press; Westport CT: Greenwood Press, 1946)

9. Quaracche II, 1008a.

10. "Tertio vero modo potesstas dominandi in homine est solum secundum statum naturae lapsae; inest enim ei secundum culpae punitionem, non secundum naturae institutionem, et hoc, quia servitus sibi correspondens, secundum quod dicunt Sancti, est poena peccati. Et quia isto modo loquimur hic de potestate dominandi, ideo concedendae sunt rationes ostendentes, quod talis potestas non inest homini secundum primarian suam conditionem sive secundum statum naturae institutae." Quaracchi II, 1008b.

11. Michael P. Malloy, *Civil Authority in Medieval Philosophy: Lombard, Aquinas andBonaventure.*(Lanham MD: University Press of America, 1985).

12. There is relevance in Bonaventure's characterization of *potestas* as *dominium*, which had long since assimilated *imperium*. A conceptual tool to liberate governance from *dominium* in personal relations, as *simplex usus facti* liberated rights discourse from *dominium* in properietary relations during the next century, as rehearsed in the chapter on Ockham, below, remains to be worked out.

13. Quaracchi II, 1008a.

14. Peter Lombard, *Sententiae in IV libris distinctae*, cura Patrum Editorum [cura Ignatii Brady, O.F.M.] (Grottaferrata [Romae] Collegii S. Bonaventurae, 1971), II, dist. 44, ch.1 (ed. Brady, 578).

15. Lombard, *Sententiae* II, dist. 44, ch.1 (ed. Brady, 578–79).

16. Malloy, *Civil Athhority in Medieval Philosophy*, 125–133.

17. "Item, rationae hoc ipsum videtur. Libertas homini inest a natura; sed potestas dominandi est libertatis impeditiva : ergo non videtur, quod sit a natura. Quod autem libertas et a natura sit et a potestate praesidendi habeat impediri, manifestatur, quia libertas sic habet definiri : 'Libertas est naturalis potestas, qua licet homini facere quod vult'. Quaracchi II, 1007b–1008a.

18. "[Christiani] propter pronitatem ad malum et concupiscentias militantes in membris, ex quibus consurgent bella et lites, ita indigent regi terreno principe sicut et alii gentes—et ideo non solum secundum humanam institutionem, sed etiam secundum divinam dispensationem inter Christianos sunt reges et principes, domini et servi—et secundem distinctionem potestatis ei subjicintur et tenentur secundum plus et minus. ... Et ideo concedendum est, quod Christiani sunt terrenis dominis obligati, non tamen in omnibus, sed in his solum, quae non sunt contra Deum; nec in his omnibus, sed in his quae secundum rectam consuetudinem rationabiliter statua sunt, sicut tributa et vectigalia et consimilia" II Sent., dist. 44, are.3, qu. 1 (ed. Quaracchi, 1011a–b).

19. See note 1.

CHAPTER NINE

SPECIFICATION OF NORM IN THE JURISPRUDENCES OF AQUINAS, AUSTIN AND KELSEN

This chapter recommends that a thomistic mode of specifying norm is more epistemically coherent and more conformed to the style of human action than either austinian or kelsenian ways. This conclusion is argued briefly after a more lengthy study of each jurisprudent's method of specifying norm, focused by very confined texts from each [1]. The study begins with a justification for forming one route into jurisprudence out of this focus and these theorists. Only some sketchy familiarity with the focal authors is presumed.

Nearly sixty years ago the prediction was made that the "pragmatist-relativist-societal emphasis" of early twentieth century legal realism and sociologism would be found wanting in our crisis age. Social, political and cultural factors would lead back to the more fundamental search for a necessary minimum value content[2]. If social fact imposes itself willy-nilly, and jurists can at best acquiesce or at worst make the implacable works less efficient, then there is nothing from which behavior can meaningfully deviate, and law is senseless.. Social fact is not normatively neutral; but to freeze law into its mold is to treat fact as though it were value-free. Although jurisprudence has not caught up with the prediction, we can feel free to look elsewhere.

We can look to Hans Kelsen, John Austin and Thomas Aquinas who each offer value as the content of law, rather than fact, Kelsen, our near contemporary and the very model of a legal phenomenologist[3], offers norm; Austin, the victorian father of analytical jurisprudence, offers command; and Aquinas, the dominant medieval natural lawyer, offers order[4]. Norm, command and order differ immensely, but share the common feature that they are demands for future behavior. They do not announce present or past occurrences, nor are they statements of conditional and perhaps causal dependency such that if event A occurs (e.g., violation; contract), then event B will occur (e.g, penalty; obligation, or penalty for non-fulfillment, according to Holmes). Kelsen is the most well-known for making this distinction of norm from fact explicit, but Austin does the same in dissociating command from "positive morality", *die Sitten* of the German romantics whom he studied. However, Aquinas does not stress this distinction, only because it was taken so much for granted in his milieu, unlike our own; because his mentality is foreign to us, Aquinas' presumptions require more detailing later than the others' do. The fact that each draws the distinction makes it possible to discuss norm in each, even if the term "norm" is purely kelsenian[5].

Once we have moved outside of those jurisprudences which are mere replicas of singular social facts, law is seen to regard not single acts but general kinds of activity. The distance between the occurrence and the norm can be narrow or wide. It is an acute problem in philosophy of action to state now even that those norms which stand shoulder to shoulder with behavior are related to it, but this is not our question[6].. Instead, our study concerns the way in which quite general norms are brought to this still problematic proximity with action. It is clear that in any legal system there are general norms which insufficiently characterize the concrete acts that either fulfill or deviate from these norms. Long before deciding whether this particular act is or is not an instance of response to this particular norm, it is necessary to state the more general norms with greater specificity.

Our three theorists have different analyses of how this is done. And because this activity is a significant moment in a legal system, a study of their variations here can serve as an entry point into the entire jurisprudence of each, and can foster an initial and perspectival judgment upon each.

AQUINAS

The claim that good is to be done is the most universal principle of practical reason for Thomas Aquinas. This claim is exposed to the essential features of human nature. The good for social human is to be done, the good for rational human is to be done, and so forth. By further identifying the social person, the corporeal person, etc., it is possible to decide ever more specifically what is the good to be done.

It is possible to specify the norm in this way because the norm is not alien to fact. For it to be a fact than an individual exists, be must be of some kind, because its existence is limited. And the kind that one is, is not an imposition of some knower' s mental categories upon one but is rather an imposition of one's reality upon the knower. One cannot be recognized simply as a presence, free of all characterization; his presence remains unperceived as long as it cannot be picked out by kind from his environment.

Because the specifications of the human person belong to his reality rather than his perceiver's reality, they can have impact upon his existence rather than being restricted to an abstract implication from concept to concept. Since any one of his determinations both opens up a set of possible developments as available to existence of his sort, and closes off others as available only to other modes of existence, his specifications are not only descriptive of the kind of existence he is but are also normative and prescriptive of the kind of behavior open to him. The human person becomes what he is able to be; and what he is both delimits a range of possible development and leads him on to his most fit development.

It is dangerous to say that such specifications are "facts"; however, this is why it was denied in the introduction and affirmed in this section that these specifications are facts. They are facts insofar as they are statements of the real kind of existence which the human person is; they are not facts insofar as they are not expected to be the behavior of all human persons we encounter. Aquinas considers that the sort of existence the human person is, is one free to realize or not her own nature, i.e., by acting so as to secure or endanger this freedom. But it is possible for her to fail; her freedom is not so unconditioned that by exercising it she will be right, no matter what, and thereby lose the responsibility for her acts which makes her freedom real. She is not a thing like other things, but she has a nature as do things, a nature to be realized differently because of being different from others.

This is the status held by specifications of human existence, and so by specifications of the most general norm of practical reason. Among these, the sociality which is one facet of the human is not an additional distinct feature added to the rest. It is interpenetrated by the others. The human is social only because she is bodily, is rational and so forth. The converse is also true, that our rationality is social in that the other is its first object of knowledge, not the self. Thus there is no conflict in advance between the good for man and the good for social man, or between moral and legal life.

To summarize up to this point, Aquinas specifies legal norms by supplying fact. This fact is not the object solely of occasional observation, nor is it the analysis of hypotheses, but is fact which is dependent upon the nature of the being whose facts, and whose norms, they are. Aquinas' procedure for specifying norm is deductive in the sense that "good is to be done" serves as a major premise while the minor premises are the specifications of good by citing what is good for man; norms specified further and further are the conclusions.

This, however, is only the first stage in Aquinas' specification of law. The deductive process does reach an end, at which some other device must be found to concretize norm further. The deduction ends not because the properties of the human person have been exhausted, leaving no more minor premises, but because of the very wealth of these human possibilities. In the deductive stage, the properties of persons needed only to be stated affirmatively, for their negative alternatives were their contradictories and so were clearly excluded. But now what appear as the alternatives are compossible and equally good because equally actualizing for alternative human potentialities. Deduction ceases when its riches overwhelm it. What it leaves behind are a range of values which are not prescribed by norm, but which instead equally satisfy it, or at least appear to fall within its permits.

What sort of legal validity has this specification which moves beyond deduction? On the one hand, to fortify a mere option among equally justifiable alternatives with the same kind of backing by deductive necessity that has fortified it to this point would court ridicule. On the other hand, the deduction is still so far from the final concrete rules of judges, administrators and legislators that to stop the force of natural law now would be to make of it a triviality and an irrelevant nuisance in the daily life of the law.

Aquinas' route from here is difficult to grasp and ambiguous. Once having exhausted conclusions from principles, then it is possible to "determine" the "common principles", as "in the arts, common forms are determined to some particular. Thus the craftsman needs to determine the common form of a house to the shape of this or that particular house". The validation this mode gives to law is uncertain; it is "derived" from natural law and in turn from eternal law and thus it does bind in conscience; but at the same time this "has no other force than that of human law". We need to know what the terms here mean, "determine" and "common form", and especially the way in which Aquinas understands an artist or craftsman at work.

"Common form" is a pleonasm; all form it potentially common to many. Aquinas is not distinguishing it from the singular form urged later by John Duns Scotus, a form which picks out the individual within his species. The common form is an epistemic reality; it is what is conceptually comprehensible in the individual existent. Especially when common form is not yet incarnated in any body other than in its images, as it is for the artist beginning his work, the work done upon it must also have some epistemic character. It is intelligent work, work of reason; this is why such results can still be "derived" from natural law, though only by "determination" and not by "conclusion".

We can further comprehend the intelligent activity of determination by playing upon Aquinas' example of the housebuilder. When he determines a common form of house to the shape of this or that house, this is different from the determination of the common form of an animate species to an individual living being of that species. The form of house can be abstracted from houses, just as the form of duck from ducks; but the procedure for using the notion is different between the two. Although it is creative to call a newly perceived instance "duck" or "house", this is far different; we can make the artifact and not the duck. I can make only what depends upon me, but neither the genesis of biological species nor the object of perception depend on me. Since the object to be made depends upon my knowledge, it gently urges the maintenance of that knowledge. To try to act unconditionally, irrespective of the epistemic reality of the common form, irrationally, is to try something impossible; the development of the artist's creative force is specified to one among the various focuses only by his knowledge, not by any natural selection.

Even more, the common form of the art object is not limited to its location in the mind or imagination of the artist. The form she particularizes is already limited by the sort of material which allows the embodiment of it in an image. The brick house has possibilities and limitations different from the stone house, long before it becomes singular, Smith's brick house as against Jones' brick house. Even before the form is brought to grips with the unevenness of Smith's back lot or the nearby highway or the building laws, in fact even before it is decided whether it shall be cottage or bungalow, duplex or semi-detached, the image that it shall be brick has already given its initial determinations.

A common form might be determinable with utter unconditionality only where it exists in purely functional definition. For example, a house is to provide shelter and to make affection resonate, in Aristotle; but as he pointed out regarding the same example, this is a rhetorical definition, not the metaphysician's expression of hylomorphic existence Yet already there are some materials better able to perform these functions than others: bamboo in the heat or in lands of minimal privacy, granite in the cold and in close-vested cultures, and water for hardly anyone below the Arctic Circle.

The point of these excursions is that the craftsman is already confined while assisted in how he determines the common form to particulars by the required materials; at no point is he disconnected from at least a bare imaginative involvement. Consequently, he is never fully distant from demands of nature, ones which he must meet or else fail. The same is true of the legal craftsman for Aquinas: although there is no imperative from the side of the public to be served after deductivity has been exploited, there remain demands from the side of the material he has to work with, social though it is. Being social it is able to be adapted to his use instead of insisting solely upon his adaptation to it. If he does this, he succeeds and does well; if he does not, he fails and also acts towards an effect contrary to natural law and thus immoral.

Aquinas identifies norm with the order deriving from the essential dynamics of human development. This order proceeds first by deduction of the necessary boundary norms from the primary norm, and then by the rational execution of the possibilities established within those bounds.

AUSTIN

John Austin seems at first not to have had the same problem at all, in fact to have been incapable of sharing such a problem. Just as a principle of individualization is no issue for metaphysicians who admit the reality only of particulars, and the difficulty becomes one of explaining how we generalize covering laws over singulars, so the specification of norm would seem to be no issue for jurisprudents who admit only of commands, or norms already concretely specified towards actions.

Austin, however, does have an analogous problem. Aquinas cannot admit of law unless it is legitimated or not invalidated by natural law, while Austin cannot recognize law unless it is possible to specify all who apply it. Austin requires a criterion to distinguish positive law from what is moral (and thus improperly positive) law. He supplies as this criterion the determinate group; even the requirement of sanction, though it supplies the command backed by force we easily take to be austinian law, is not as ultimate as this.

The determinate group is a class of individuals, all of whom can be specified as belonging to that group; all others can be specified as not belonging to that group and therefore not subject to its laws. Of everyone one meets, he can say "You are in" or "You are out". The description of the group is the criterion for membership, and thus of concretely specified law.

So far, like Aquinas: the description specifies the norm. But it is from sources other than that description that norm becomes law. It is not because the nature of this group requires this or that. Once the group is determined, the content of the norms falling upon the group in command is not derived from the characterizing features of the group. Instead, the content is irrelevant to the norm being or not being law; all that is required is that the content be such that it is able to be applied over all. If either the class of subjects to whom the command is given or the class of acts so commanded contains only one individual, or is even null, this is still law. This remains true provided that the subject and his acts are described by features which maintain their class membership, rather than by their proper names, even if that class identity is such that by definition the class can contain but one member. All that is excluded is singular or particular commands applied to an individual or group for only one particular instance.

Command is immediately concrete; it specifies the act to be performed, not solely the class of acts. If the command is not in a form fit for ready compliance, if it is ambiguous, the subject resolves this best by asking for the precise behavioral directives intended.

There is no hint in Austin that the class of acts referred to by norm must be so empirical that it includes only those acts which have occurred, such that the norm is a shorthand for those acts. Command is clearly intended to have reference to future acts. But the difficulties of describing these future acts in detail in any other way are not dealt with when Austin places command as the essence of law, with no question raised of such law's content.

We must return, then, to Austin's discussion of the subject of norm, since there is no room given us by him to discuss the content of norm. The demand for a determinate body is a demand not upon the recipient of command but upon the commander. It is a device to distinguish the command that is law from the common opinion or the social custom or even the social morality that is not law. Law cannot issue from an indeterminate group because such a group is incapable of forming or intimating a wish as a body. As Austin says, indeed such a group may "regard" some action as desirable or not and in fact may be "displeased" with those who vary from their regard, and consequently even be able to visit evil upon the victim of displeasure. But it is unable to form or express a "wish" which is the essential material of command and thus of law.

This distinction Austin draws between wish and regard is not developed by him. But it does lie at the bottom of the sovereign's ability to command; and since that ability contains the immediate specification of norm, it is essential to try and penetrate the distinction.

The distinction appears to be that the acts belong respectively to knowledge and to volition. It seems to be Austin's view that the two domains of human activity are distinct in that volition does and knowledge does not require a unity in the human person so active. Having developed no epistemology nor psychology independent of his jurisprudence, Austin does not make available any materials on these activities in the individual person. A sovereign unified in an individual person, rather than a group, may also take up an attitude towards a form of behavior and may form a wish in regard to it. Both activities proceed from the same active center. When a group takes up such an attitude, .its activity emerges from many disparate sources, each turning upon the behavior his own estimate. The effect is for this to remain an individual initiative both when formed and when expressed, so that any sanctions which follow upon such a regard are the work of individuals. However, if the group so regarding is formed into a whole by a common description or by all having like features, their regard proceeds from the fact that they are of such a kind, with such a direction. They can project from a present and inert response a line of conduct for the future, and form a wish that it be followed, something which requires an initiative and consequently a more centered unity of energy that the mere formation of a presently responsive attitude.

Austin offers two modes of characterizing the deteminacy of bodies able to wish. These characterizations throw light on the nature of the wishing that they can perform, and thus upon the specification of norm of which they are capable. The first way of distinguishing a determinate body is by picking out a feature of each person which belongs to him rather than to a genus. This characterizes him, and this is what makes him the member of the group. This is one way of determining each member.

Unfortunately the examples given do not resolve all questions about this. At one extreme of interpretation, the group could be found composed of members with nothing in common but that each had been named a member. This would closely approach a mathematical set, wherein the members of the set have no features in common but being members of the set. It is possible to specify all of the members by giving their names, beginning at the. first and going to the last. Their individual names are what allow judgment about whether or not this individual is a member; scan the list to ascertain whether the individual appears upon it.

The second way of distinguishing a determinate body is more essentialist. A group will contain as members all the individuals of a certain kind. Austin's phrasing clearly means that here it is the descriptive feature of a class which precedes selection of the individuals making it up. Picking out individuals by their possession of a class characteristic forces admission of all who bear that characteristic. Since the description is what precedes selection in this manner of selection, it cannot be refused in individual instances.

The structure of members of the determinate groups, then, is that they bear both individual designations and generic descriptions, either one of which may be employed to determine the group. One may proceed by assigning all the persons in it, or else by indicating every person in it. These ways appear to be exclusive alternatives rather than alternative descriptions of the same determination. Since what is being determined is a body of persons fit to give commands and so fit to be a center of energy for wishing, the authority to issue command is not present in the very determining of that group; Austin does not consider the likelihood of the determinate group determining itself, although he does not exclude it. The most, then, that could be determined by the second method would be a superior, though not a sovereign. The sovereign could make the determination of those bodies known as superiors, but not superiors the determination of their own sovereign.

The makeup of members must therefore be equally divided between individuality and specificity, what is named and what it described. Indeed, the final purpose of the latter way of assigning members is, in turn, that they may be named, every one. A structure of the individual in which individuality can be named, and named in some way different from the description and in which this naming will form a group fit to make wishes and commands, is a structure of existence wherein the common form really is set over against individual form. The individual form offers the privacy which sharing solely of a common form does not, a staging platform for vigorous initiative or actions which stand on their bare fact of existence alone rather than upon their being a concretization of what is abstractly acceptable.

KELSEN

For Hans Kelsen, much more frankly than Aquinas or Austin, the problem of jurisprudence is the problem of how to specify norm. While Aquinas' search for unity in law is carried out so as to manifest the coherence in providence, and while Austin's project is launched so as to achieve clarity of distinction between overlapping and blurred boundaries at the edges of domains in human behavior, Kelsen for his part is directly interested in stressing the fact that law cannot exist at all unless it exists as a system. The relevant sort of system is a *system* of validations, wherein the characteristic ideality is one of oughtness. To express it without undue awe, out of the big ought are generated little oughts, or at least the little ones can have their parentage dignified by genetic research. The manner of specifying norm is the very heart of his theory.

As his project is more frankly to our purposes, so he more frankly admits his way of carrying it out. While a norm system may be based upon acts of intellection, the norm system of law is founded on acts of will. Kelsen calls the former a static system of norms, the latter a dynamic one. The reason for this terminology is that specification of norm by intellectual act does no more than reveal what is already present from the outset in the basic norm, while the latter way has no content given in full from the start but only initiates activity

The reason why Kelsen ties law to dynamic rather than static norm systems is that the feature of law which differentiates it from other sorts of systems, i.e., norm, is found more ideally pure where fact does not enter as the vehicle bearing norm; oughtness which stands most unadulterated or uncompromised gives the clearest vision of law. Not just empirical fact, but even the analysis of content which claims to be conceptual is improper and deceptive so norm must be founded in norm alone.

Nonetheless, Kelsen yields what he considers to be major concessions on the static character even of dynamic systems. First, there is some content to the dynamic system, a minimum content to be prescribed; only, this content is not the dynamism of law. Again, "the application of general norm to the concrete case involves the same intellectual operation as the deduction of an individual from a general norm of natural law"; but the application of general to individual is not the same as the specification of general into less general. And, finally, the basic norm itself "is not itself made, but is a hypothetical, presupposed norm; it is not positive law, but only its condition. .... Its validity is assumed by virtue of its contents ..." and, as a result, it is "valid, then, like a norm of natural law."

It is because the basic norm grants authority to impose specific norms that law reaches down to the concrete norms. While holding that static norm systems apply law to the concrete case by deduction (all A ought to y; you are A; so y), Kelsen insists that more general dynamic norms are specified in some other way. That way is by an exercise of will. He does not exclude, but rather insists that accompanying this will-act as its object is a content which does derive rationally from more general contents. In this he distinguishes himself from the procedural (or "technological," as Passerin d'Etrèves calls it) natural law of Lon Fuller, for whom the statements about how authority should be exercised form the very heart of natural law principles.

Unlike Austin and like Aquinas, then, Kelsen acknowledges the presence of a content of norm persisting through its gradual specification. Unlike Aquinas and like Austin, however, it is not the intelligible content which explains and justifies that specification but rather it is the acts of will which do this. The reason for insisting upon this is stated above, as being the ideality of oughtness. As in his frankness thus far, Kelsen again frankly acknowledges a kantian epistemology to be at the basis of this: oughtness in acts of will is the contact with reality which analytic intellectual derivation misses, remaining in the order of appearances. The logic which accompanies this is that the basic "ought" is specified by having the subject of its propositional formula specified rather than its object. Instead of "A ought to x" being specified more closely by defining the object down to "A ought to y", the kelsenian specification runs "B ought to x". What gets specified is the "determinate body" of Austin, specified from a higher authority to a lower authority; thereby the oughtness of the norm stays untouched and the law persists faithful to its ideality.

The will of authority is exercised upon its properly confined object in the course of delegation. If we can imagine Kelsen's system as actively running down the ranks, from basic norm to ordinary norm, as well as running for research purposes back up the ranks, from ordinary to basic, then what authority authorizes is authority. Even the most derived norm can be so viewed: the concrete statute or decision authorizes the placing of penalty or of some accomplishment upon specified behavior rather than excluding or demanding that behavior. This is to reduce all of Hart's "primary rules" into his "secondary rules", which is the work carried out in detail by some of the Scandanavian realists in a tradition partially derivative from Kelsen. The will of authority is confined within the proper scope of authority: authorizing.

What is essential for Kelsen's technique to work is that it be, first of all, possible. It is the possibility of the pure will-act upon which such a jurisprudence must rest. Will must be an ultimate category of human activity, if not the ultimate category. Willing must be not only irreducible to another activity or component of activity; it must also not be conditioned by any other form of activity. It must be both causally and logically independent.

The conclusion of this study will make some references to the possibility for so acting, without a detailed attempt to justify what is referred to. What I will suggest will be some informal and vague criteria for making evaluations of the jurisprudences discussed.

CONCLUSION

One common thrust of all breeds of recent philosophy—existential, analytical, marxist, pragmatist—has been their refusal of cartesian mentalism. The knower is no longer assumed to have the ability to begin her sojourn from an ego independent of her body and, therefore, of her society. The main critique has been that the knower would be unable to have access not only to others' minds but even to his own. Only to the extent he could be available to others could he be available to himself, since he meets himself in self-consciousness not as a transparently self-reflected whole but as isolated into the poles of a mediated relationship to himself: I and me.

This critique will not be rehearsed at greater length, for it is everywhere at hand. Despite countermoves by returning toward kantian separation of science and morals, knowing and willing, the overall direction has been to replace bodiliness into mental events.

Bodiliness has not functioned as a univocal criterion but instead has splintered into myriad shards because of its ubiquitous presence. Among the perspectives based upon it would be the refusal to acknowledge any antiseptic knowledge value-free and purposeless; because bodily dependency necessitates the omnipresence of self-interest, mental acts must be penetrated by willfulness. In turn, since the "mental acts" encompass not just acts of knowledge but any hidden psychic events, acts of will are also taken to be mental acts and so are outcast. To rehabilitate them, pure will acts are to be seen as penetrated by knowledge of ends and means. In summary, the critique reintegrates knowledge and will.

The attempt to design a rationale for the specification of legal norm by our three jurisprudents can be brought to this bar for critique. Austin and Kelsen's forthright separation of acts of will commanding or authorizing from knowledge acts appears to cripple their methodology immediately; it demands of people what people cannot do. Aquinas' two-storeyed mode of specification seems to have more to recommend it, for it includes one storey of intellect and another of will, both essential to the legal process. But this is inadequate insofar as it requires two sets of impossible acts instead of one, rather than melding the two into one integral whole.

However, the route out would be to recognize what was stressed regarding the level of "determination" in Aquinas, that the artistic model demands rather than repels rationality. Also, in regard to the first level, that of "conclusion", the characteristics which are deduced are not mental modifications of the knower. They are the core of the known, which drive it toward its own development which integrate its dynamism into others' ends and means.

On balance, then, Aquinas offers a more feasible way of specifying norm. Since this point is a key one to jurisprudence, this conclusion suggests a prejudice in regard to the entirety of each of these jurisprudences. As in all cases of philosophy, the upshot of this is to try and offer some way of understanding and making possible what we do in fact perform, rather than to alter behavior. In any case, norm does get specified; our argument for Aquinas is not to say that norm should be specified as he analyzes, but rather to say that it is done that way. The only norm this chapter offers is one identified with the essential facts of human action.

NOTES

1. Thomas Aquinas.. *Summa theologiae*, IaIIae, q. 95, a.2 [1272], in *Aquinas: Selected Writings*, ed. A. P. D'Entrèves, trans. J. G,,.Dawson (Oxford: Blackwell, 1970). Pp. 128–129; John Austin, *The Province of Jurisprudence Determined*, Lecture V [1832], intro. H..L.A,.Hart (London; Weidenfeld and Nicolson, 1955), pp. 141, 144–146; Hans Kelsen, *The Pure Theory of Law*, trans. Max Knight from 2nd German ed. [1960; 1st ed.,1934] Berkeley: University of California Press, 1967), pp. 195, which continues by not explicitly modifying (as his text does so frequently) his position *in General Theory of Law and State*, trans. Anders Wedberg (1945); and the selection from his *Die philosophischen Grundlagen der Naturrechtslehre und des Rechtpositivismus* [1929], trans. W.K. Krause, as edited in *The Nature of Law* by M. P. Golding (New York: Random House, 1966), pp. 124.

2. Edward McWhinney, "Legal Theory and Philosophy of Law In Canada," in *Canadian Jurisprudence; The Civil Law and Common Law in Canada*, ed. McWhinney (Toronto: Carswell, 1958), p. 19.

3. Cf. Paul Amselek's *Méthòde phéoménologique et théorie du droit* (Paris, 1964).

4. The ambiguity of "order" between "direction", "pattern" and "coherence" is systematic, as shall appear.

5. The alternative to using such a term would be to employ such a clumsy formal term as "deontic enunciation" to cover all three usages, since alternative simple terms do not suffice; e.g . "modal" applies to too wide a spectrum of modes, "rule" or "imperative" are too limited to the austinian doctrine, "standard" or "principle" objectify what is not so fully objectified in all our authors.

6. The perversion of legal realism in this respect lies beyond the scope of this study. Suffice it to say that its models in the positivistic enterprise of nineteenth century physical science have been the main enemy of its critics.

CHAPTER TEN

OCKHAM ON TRUSTS

The medieval English friars used goods by means of a distinctive legal instrument, namely, by the use. This is different from their continental brothers' means, the tools of civilian law, although it depended upon the civilian court of chancery for enforcement. The friars were the first to employ uses in a widespread manner[1]. But this was developed into English common law's most significant contribution to the holding of property, the legal trust.

Given that the English friars of the thirteenth century were recognized both as the most observant of their brethren, and also as the most scholarly[2], it would be surprising if these characteristics developed apart. One would expect the poor brothers' holdings to be grist for the learned brothers' philosophy, since property holding served more than anything else as a norm for their group identity. No explanation would be needed for this occurring. But to explain why it did not, if such were the case, would require torturous indirection to locate denial, defensiveness or shame which turned the friars' attention off of themselves. Such diffidence about their vocation was not one of their faults.

Did they attend to their employment of the trust? The trust properly so called, or the use upon a use, does not appear until the sixteenth century, and then as a response to the Crown's remedies for the losses of revenue which uses brought about. But of course by then the English friars' fame for observance and for scholarship had passed, anyway.

In the thirteenth and fourteenth centuries, however, with which we are concerned in this chapter, Adam Marsh, Robert Grosseteste, Alexander Hales, John Pechham and Roger Bacon can be expected to reflect upon their property norms as well in their moral philosophies as in their defences of poverty. Curiously, this does not seem to have occurred. Less surprise would be occasioned by the fact of a continental Bonaventure not so reflecting on English property tools, or even a Duns Scotus who would have experienced them later than scotists' civilian tools.

But any overt reflection is hard to find even in Ockham where we would most expect it, having been both born and bred to the use, and being plunged into property law on the other hand.

Since no explicit discussion of the English use has been found in Ockham, the only way to develop even a framework of plausibility for the initial expectation is to examine the state of development which the use had reached by the time of Ockham. By seeing whence this state of the use had come, it can be tested whether this could have led to Ockham's understanding of property. And by seeing whither the use was going, it can be tested whether this could have been moved along by Ockham's understanding of property.

Even if the case can be made in this way, it remains only conjectural. In order for it to approach demonstrativeness, other explanations for both Ockham's thinking and for the development of the use must be set aside. But each has already been explained in terms of other factors; so demonstration is an unlikely goal.

What might bring it closer is an awareness on the part of the friars' superiors or their patrons that the property transactions they were undertaking needed to be understood in terms akin to those that the friar-philosophers were using. More of this in closing.

The origins of the use are not perspicuous because, on the one side, it is not derived from non-English models and, on the other, it is in no great evidence until the friars use it as an already well developed instrument. Its homegrown nature is both its pride and its frustration.

The use is an arrangement whereby goods are transferred from one person to a second person for a third person's benefit. "A to B for the use of C", is its schematic formula. This is dissimilar to any of the fragmentary rights of property known under Roman law, since the middle person drops from civilian rights both of use and of usufruct, while real servitude requires both a dominant and a servient immoveable. It is also dissimilar to civilian *negotiorum gestio*, or the management of another's property, because this arises only when the first person is unwilling, and his property remains his own. Civilian models handle relations only between two persons.[3]

As well, the attempt to locate an origin in Germanic customary law has failed, although it has enjoyed a lively history. The closest model was the *salman* whom a departing warrior made the administrator of his property. This role as executor does not fit, since the second party to the use does not just administer but owns the goods. Nor are goods in the use to pass over to the third eventually.[4]

The three parties to the trust are called the donor, the donee or trustee, and the beneficiary. In the feudal law of uses these parties are called the feoffor, the feoffee to uses, and the cestui que use, as a shorthand term. Here the terms donor, donee and beneficiary will be employed despite their anachronism.

The earliest examples of uses appear before the 800s in the Carolingian kingdom[5] But the expanded use is nearly simultaneous with the friars' entry into England in 1224, the year after their new Rule. While Bracton recites a steward's receipt of money for his employer's use a year earlier than that, his first group of secular examples come from several years later, 1225–26: a knight off to the crusades puts his land in another's hands for his sons' use, and this other is held to deliver it; a father buys the land of his daughter's fiancee and holds it for the son-in-law's use, who then has both land and money; a creditor takes his debtor's land and holds it to this debtor's use, as a security on the debt. The Yearbook from the reign of Henry VII cites no sources for pushing the use further back into the reign of Henry II as the time when uses first began to be enforced against reluctant feoffees by the Chancellor for the donee's failure to perform. But surely by 1238 the question is being raised whether the donee holds for his own use, the donor's or the use of his mother who is beneficiary.

The formula used in these early secular examples is to deal with lands *ad opus*: the donor commits these to the donee for the beneficiary's *opus*, translated as "use". The first approximations to the term "use" is at the end of the thirteenth century, in 1293, and again in 1305, when the law-French *a la oeus* and *al oes* appear. However, even in secular affairs an ordinary formula is the gerund(ive): *ad custodiendum ad opus*, or *ad disponiendum et venditioni exponiendum* in the 1230s.[6]

Among the friars, this gerundive construction is used almost exclusively.[7] The many deeds kept of their London houses, in particular, speak of giving *pro inhabitatione* and *ad inhospitandum*. Only in 1262 do two with the phrase *in usus fratrum minorum* appear; and none thereafter. Fifteen years earlier, the king had ordered the sheriff to receive a house *ad opus* of the friars, after the mayor had given the house to the king *ad amplificationem* of the friars' dwellings. Besides this, the only other deeds *ad opus* were the very first house, belonging to Robert le Muliner, in 1224; and another in 1282 giving the rental income from a house for the friars' *opus*. Here the ambiguity stands out between *opus* as a term of art, and as a reference to their mission work.

This form of donation was used not only for houses and lots, but also for chattels, particularly money gifts and, as just seen, the civil fruits of property for their support. No deeds survive for the donation of consumables. This is hardly surprising, since simple transfer is all that was needed to convey them. But it is of interest insofar as the dispute in which the friars became engaged regarding poverty had to do mostly with their ownership of consumables, not of their dwellings. Although no documents do reflect this, the treatment of money as a consumable in the papal dispute, and its treatment by the deeds in the same manner as immoveables, may bridge the gap.

The nature of the object donated for the friars becomes increasingly clear to the donors. In the last fifteen years of the thirteenth century, three deeds cease speaking of giving lands or income, and instead donate all the *ius* which the donors have in their buildings. While this is not a complete turnabout from a naturalistic idea of the gift to a legalistic one, since donors had earlier guaranteed (*warrantizabimus*) and secured good title (*quietum clamavit*) on their property to the friars, it does show a new level of awareness at the turn of the century, as the debate heated up.

The most noteworthy feature of deeds to the friars, is that almost without exception the gifts for friars are made to a public body, most characteristically to the *communitas civium Londiniae*. The gift is often made by a public person, the king or mayor or the queen. The donee is not the papacy, unlike the continental gifts. Not only does this mean that the responsibilities and deserts of both parties are closer at hand, but also that the relevant law for the friars is not the civilian law of the papacy on the continent. Whatever is the development of English law in regard to the use, it is also that which affects the English friars. Whether they also contribute to it is a question for this study.

The chief question to be answered as to the legal nature of uses is what were the rights and duties of the three parties over the times at which the use developed. Could the beneficiary or the donor take action against a donee who refused to employ the gift in the intended way?[8] Given this, it will be easier to see when if at all Ockham's social philosophy has impact upon it.

The structure of uses required that the donee was the owner, and only the rights of this owner could be pursued at common law. The land did not belong to the beneficiary, nor did it any longer belong to the donor. Suits upon a contract still lay centuries in the future. But since the donee had promised or "plighted faith", the chancellor who had until recently been an ecclesiastic would hear the case for a *laesio fidei*. While his courts could enforce no order as to the disposition of the estate, they could order the imprisonment of defendants who acted in contempt of their orders. This was the situation as far back as the reign of Henry II in the twelfth century.

The last quarter of the thirteenth century was a time more for the statutory control of mortmain. Land put into a religious tenure no longer owed the incidents of tenure to the king, nor would it ever owe them again since the religious order which held it was perpetual. This concerned the monks, not the friars, who did not hold any tenure at all and whose donees held with ordinary tenures.

In mid-fourteenth century, reentry by the donor was deemed to be a sufficient remedy against a disloyal donee. The first case of use was heard by the chancellor in 1350. The first will to uses is noted in 1355. In the last quarter of the century, the first statutes are legislated under Richard II to prevent frauds upon creditors: land conveyed in mortmain to others for the debtor's use were made liable for execution. Parliament also continued to answer that the common law would not enforce the use. Towns were made as perpetual as orders, so that they could not hold in perpetuity for the friars' use. Uses were made as forfeitable for treason, as were the various forms of tenure.

In the fifteenth century, uses ceased being a situation, and became an institution. This occurred by the increasingly frequent bills brought to the courts of equity, after Parliament's repeated failure to act upon the Common's "prayer" that it remedy the donee's right to alienate the property in denial of the beneficiary's use. By the latter half of the century, this personal remedy of the beneficiary was made available to his heir and to a buyer. The beneficiary's alienation of the property was made valid against all challenges; those of the donee were not so secured. The heir of a beneficiary who died intestate was made liable for paying the feudal incidents again.

In the sixteenth century, the same curtailment that was administered earlier to mortmain was given to uses. Lands held in use could be executed for the beneficiary's debts; in order to do so, he received all the rights and duties as if it were his legal estate. This is exactly what several bills do in the 1530s: "execute" the use by placing the full estate onto the beneficiary; require every use to be publicly registered; and levy feudal dues on both the donee's and the beneficiary's estates. At the same time, unincorporated groups like .the friars were restricted from being beneficiaries of any use longer than twenty years. As compensation for these losses, beneficiaries won the right to will lands freely.

Only in the last part of that century did the common law courts permit a means for avoiding these restrictions. This instrument was what developed from the use, by then ineffectual, into the trust properly so called, namely, the use upon a use. Its formula is a gift "from A to the use of B to the use of C". The second use, if not executed, could accomplish the same as the earlier use, e.g., if "from A to the use of B to the use of A". This device is first refused by chancery as contrary to the common law, then later is accepted by it as unexecuted when it concerns a lease, and finally by the early seventeenth century is accepted for all purposes. From then on, the trust exists.

So while the question eventually becomes one of how to avoid frauds by the beneficiary, the question in the thirteenth and fourteenth century is how the beneficiary can get enforcement of the use against a faithless "trustee". It is just this upon which Ockham's approach to property turns.

The gist of the situation is that while Ockham must struggle to convince Romanists of a use without suit, it is commonplace in the legal system he knows best. Ockham is not alone in his argument, for he follows nearly a century of battle, much of which was carried out by men from the continent and. its Romanist systems. They knew that was what they wanted; but they did not succeed. Authorities suggest they were wrong and Pope John XXII was right: there was no room for such a notion within Roman law.[9] If it is to be founded in law, it must be on something other than continental civilian systems.

In turn, the limitations Ockham puts on how the use can be manipulated look toward the future development of the use in.English law. The gradual acquisition of recovery, later, by the beneficiary, indeed the execution of all the rights of use upon him, goes beyond what friar-practitioners of the use found desirable and did exactly what John wanted. But the emergence yet later of the use upon a use, now with increased protection for the beneficiary, does approach what Ockham was driving after.

It is clear, then, that there is in English law some act of using in which the beneficiary is unprotected. Ockham's task is to make it appear that there is some comparable way of using things in civilian law, or to create one.

Ockham's argument must first show that there can exist this unprotected use at all, one which brings no rights on the part of the user. But secondly, he must show that the friars do not foist upon the legal order an uncertainty in the holding of property; for their use, while it brings no rights to the user, does bring duties upon the donor or the donee, duties which can be enforced in just the way English uses could, whether it be friars or others who trigger that process.[10]

The purely verbal dimension of this can be addressed by asking whether Ockham uses the discourse peculiar to the English deeds of use, and whether this is distinctive from civilist instruments, or not.

The most distinctive terminology of *ad opus* is not apparent. Ockham's employment of the word is in the commonplace sense of Acts 4: 35, *unicuique dividebatur prout opus erat*, "according to his need" (9: 35, 46).[11] A usage more technical, but still underdetermined, regards friars' incapacity to sue for their use. Christ forbids lawsuits, not only because of the worry, but also *quantum ad opus, quantum ad operis executionemn* (116: 195–973, 22; 115: 57–58). This is simply a function of the grammatical construction, not a vehicle for conceptual change.

The gerundive usage with *ad* or *in*, both common in deeds of English use, is found freely through Ockham, e.g., *domus ad inhabitandum* (2: 154). But this usage is common through the Roman law of property, too. His loose use of *dare* as *ministrare, tradere* rather than as a transfer of dominium or ownership, accords with the deeds but is not distinctive (103: 100–2). Similar observations can be made about reference to donors as not only *donantes* but also *concedentes, patroni* or *fundatores* (77: 185, 200, 207). And the term *aequitas naturalis* (65: 76–80), while tempting to read with reference to English equity, could be so read only with gross anachronism.

Of the central term, *usus,* Ockham's discussion is manifold. While he does not want to be accused of logic-chopping (preface: 17–18), still he advises those unskilled in the art to steer clear of the debate (95: 492–94), because of the distinctions which need to be grasped. Unfortunately, the phrase *ad usum* to which Ockham addresses himself so much, is not the phraseology of the deeds of English use, which instead run *ad opus*.Also, they are not in the plural, *ad usus*

Christ did not have even his sandals *ad usum*, in the sense of a right (94: 50, 125). But he had his clothing *quantum ad usum, quoad usum* (94: 290, 323, 333; 117: 88). But, worse yet for any distinctiveness, it is both the Vulgate that speaks of *in usum quotidianum utatur* (2: 98–105), and Roman law itself which speaks of *ad usum quotidianum utatur* (42: 20).[12]

While it is certainly not to his purpose to point out that his terminology is distinctive, Ockham at least wishes to make it precise. The noun *usus* is broader than the verb *uti*. While the verb is employed only in the sense of the act of using, the noun is employed in that sense plus many others. Ockham slides away from concluding that "Friars have no *usus*" implies "Friars have no *uti licite*," by comparing it with the nonsense of concluding from *Nullus bonus utatur divinatione* to *Nullus bonus est divinus* (3: 581–90). *Uti* employed in this way, though not found in Scripture as referring to the friars' sort of use, is not contrary to Scripture; and is in fact found in the popes' writings (56). Finally, the friars' detractors commonly employ the term in just the way the friars intend it, even in the course of denying it. For in saying that the friars must have *usus rerum usu consumptibilium*, the detractors deny in the first employment of the term what they affirm in the second; all the friars want is that same *usus* by which things are consumed, whereas their detractors deny there is any such use unprotected by law (37: 60–65). Even in law, *uti* mostly means the act of using; that it means both this, and the legal right, makes it equivocal, not univocal (37: 105–8).

The use in which friars are interested is not *usus iuris*, "quodam ius positivum determinatum, institutun, ex ordinatione humana, quo quis habet licitam potestatem et auctoritatem uti rebus alienis, salva rei substantia" (2: 127–30).[13] Whether a bare use by which one can use things for his family living but not deal with the things (3: 443–65)[14], or a usufruct in which one can sell the right, both of these *usus iuris* involve a litigible right (3: 130–54).

So also does *ius utendi*, "potestas licita utendi re extrinsica quo quis sine culpa sua et absque causa rationabili privari non debet invitus, et si privata fuerit, privantem potuerit in iudicio convenire" (2: 155–60).

Instead, the friars' use is an *usus facti*, the mere activity of employing an external thing (2: 98–125). It is simple use (as distinct from bare use above) in that, besides the activity of using, it involves a licit power of using, which is separate from every right which could be sued upon (6: 304–5). While this use excludes any reliance upon law to protect it, nonetheless the laws properly understood do provide room for it, rather than exhaustively determining the domain of property holdings and excluding it (49:75).

The legal category in which *usus facti* is located is that of a license, *licencia* (41: 185–90; also *licita potestas, usus licitus, uti re aliena de licencia alicuius*, 66: 297–98). In the division of *ius utendi*, it may be natural or positive, the positive may be divine or human, and the human may be either what one cannot be deprived of without having suit, or else "illud quod competit alicui solummodo ex gratia et licencia, quo non potest aliquis contra quemcumque in iudicio experiri" (60: 105–107). No one holds by divine right today (also 3: 395–400); no one can renounce natural rights; and the friars have no lawsuits. So what is permitted to them as a use is a natural right, and a human unlitigible right (60: 90–107).[15]

This is similar to a privilege, in that it is revocable at will. But it is unlike a privilege because the holders of privilege can sue third parties who try and dispossess them, even if not those who gave them the privilege. This is why privilege is called a *lex*, and a *ius*.(3: 395–414)

Instead, this license arises from a state of fact, viz., the state of necessity (65: 135–40). The friars' way of relieving themselves of any litigible rights is by bringing themselves under "necessity, which has no law" (23: 369–70). One of its distinctive features is that, when the necessity ends, the holder of the object cannot retain it any longer (3: 427–25); just as, if protected rights were not permitted to the Apostles on their missionary journeys, when they were in direst necessity, so much less would they have such rights once home again (102: 240–50). People have this right *omni tempore*, at all times; yet not *pro omni tempore*. for employment at any moment, but only in moments of necessity (61: 35–44). Yet there remains the provocative suggestion that this *ius poli*, or license in time of necessity, can be used in other situations as well (65: 191–99); or, returning to the earlier terminology, that while every necessary use is a *usus facti*, the opposite is not true (58: 110–15). This is only partly explained by noting that the limitation in time applies only to objects which belong to another, and not to unowned objects (65: 218–25).[16]

Although not protected by law, this use is not contrary to law; it is a license, *usus licitus*. Ockham goes to pains to discriminate licit use from just use, lest assimilation to the latter put it back underneath legal justice. "The act of using is licit even without a right of using." (66: 581) For "justice" has three meanings, "as treated by Aquinas": a particular virtue, alongside the other cardinal virtues; the general virtue of legal justice, which orders all acts of virtue to the common good; and a metaphorical sense, "the due ordering of acts to reason" (60: 120–59). In the first and second senses, it makes sense to say that many licit acts are not just acts; while in the third and harmless sense all of them are. This sense of justice (and the same is said of *fas* at 66: 10–50) is a "middle" sense, between the just and the unjust, which remains so by "abnegation" (also 65: 165–83).

This means simply that license is nothing but to act in a morally upright manner, *bene moraliter facere*, so the license to use is the right to use in a morally proper way, as is the license to possess (65: 181–85). This morality, however, is of an objective sort attaching to the relationship between parties; it does not go down so far as to the personal uprightness of the user. For Ockham, the friars' way of using things, even if it is illicit and contrary to the Rule, does not vary the location of the ownership at all, the dominium; though they act like owners, they do not become owners, any more than a thief would (77: 371–88). Again, with an example from property law at large, as many possess by *ius fori* who possess badly, so many possess without *ius fori* at all as do those who possess something by legitimate prescription but before the prescription has fully run (65: 391–95). These points are worthy of note insofar as they relate to limitations upon the friars' feoffees which, as we shall see, is based upon their moral obligation and not based upon the friars' moral claims, nor diminished by the friars' "unclean hands".

If the friars' use is a license which cannot be defended, it is no wonder that so many of John's claims tried to foist lawsuits upon the friars. Their refusal to accept litigious rights is set upon the Christian's avoidance of sin: it is as quasi-natural to deceive one another in carrying lawsuits, as it is in making contracts (116: 86–91). And it is as hard to avoid sin if only the other party does this, as if it is oneself (116:91–95). So Christ forbade not only the worry over lawsuits, but the very carriage of them (116: 195–97). But while he forbade violence in defense of persons and suits in defense of property to some, though not all, he did not forbid a defense by means of reason and admonition to anyone, lest property be taken away, although even here the anxieties often associated were to be avoided (117: 70–90).

To this point, the indefensible status of the friars' use is its core feature, one which mirrors the inability of any beneficiary to recover a use at English common law during this time. The second phase of investigation is to discover that the defensibility of the friars' use in other forums also parallels the beneficiary's access to the English courts of chancery.[17]

The phrase usually employed in Ockham's denial of a suit at law gives a hint of the direction: *absque culpa et causa privari non debet* (e.g., 60: 10–18) The friars can be deprived of their license; but the one who deprives them does sin, even if not against the friars. And, given the availability of enforcement machinery, the license "can attain the force of law not on the part of the principal, but on the part of the subject" (65: 75). To give an even stronger statement, it is equitable (*aequum*) that you do not prohibit me from what benefits me and does not harm you; and, even though its equitability lacks *ius fori*, still no human law can be set up against it, because that would be a wrongful (*iniqua*) law (66: 47–50).

Between them, these sweeping claims set up the basis for just such equitable enforcement against notorious sinfulness which the English chancery gave by restraining. the body of wrongdoers, i.e., imprisonment, although their property passed under the common law. What remains is to indicate the various sources whence this wrongfulness could come, and the conditions in which friars could trigger either this or, where available, common law enforcement.

The obligation of those who hold property for use of the friars arises from limitations upon their dominium. The definition of full (*plenum*) dominium is of *dominium mundanum et civile*: "potestas vel habens annexam potentiam libere vendicandi, donandi et sicut sibi placuerit disponendi res quarum habetur dominium" (4: 101–3). This is clearly, then, also free (*liberum*) dominium, since it is at one's will. As well, *dominium humanitus inventum* includes the power "per quod possit quis in judicio pro rebus temporalibus litigare" (4: 328–29). The law is at its disposal because the law defines it as "potentia alienandi, vendendi, donandi, legandi et alii ad placitum quia secundum iura civilia rerum suarum unusquisque est legitimus moderator et arbiter" (4: 649–51). The only restriction on such use is the natural law (2: 377–80).[18]

The essential feature of full dominium is to be able to do all these actions *ad libitum*. To the extent this liberty is lessened, to that extent is dominium less full, and an obligation burdens the ownership. Thus, "in many places"[19] there is more dominium over moveables, since immoveables cannot be validly sold, given or willed so as to exclude the heirs from them; if this is done, it may be deemed invalid (2: 398–414). A house, which is an immoveable, is not a consumable, i.e., it is not used up by its use except *per accidens* (2: 248–49); but many moveables are also durables, so this restriction tends to pass along to them, as well.

Since it is useful even to have the power of placing the fruits of a thing, its dominium without fruit is not useless or valueless (96: 200); but it is less. Even less is it when the dominium of goods is held for the common good of the community (4: 308–13), for the disposal of its fruit is much more confined. And clerics who hold goods in the same way as laymen have still less full dominium, because so many uses of their goods are forbidden by canon law (2: 380–90).

Still less full or free, and the more bound by obligation, is the dominium which is received with a given use attached. Clerics are even more bound, however, over goods which the faithful have offered to God, because they are held to certain ways for disposing of them. Because their dominium is so restricted, they are called *dispensatores* or *procuratores* in canon law (2: 425–32). They are constrained not just negatively, from certain use, but positively, to the positive acts of a given sort.

While Ockham does not indicate who the suitors are in that case,, donors or beneficiaries, he does so clearly in another. Several times he points out that Pope Nicholas III in the bull *Exiit qui seminat* of 1279 said expressly that he received into the *dominium* of the Roman church all things that the friars use (e.g., 2: 365); and it is not beneath her dignity to sue for even the vile and despicable goods the friars employ.[20] It is not essential to their Rule that the pope hold them; dominium of some things they employ belongs to the church, others belong to lay owners. But if the latter relinquish dominium, presumably not specifying whither it go, then the goods go to the church. Whether it does so is indifferent to the friars, for they use the goods as abandoned things. But for these many houses and objects to be so devoid of owners and so of security, "hoc tamen minime reipublicae expediret" (77: 330–45). So the very reason the church takes them, is to have the exclusive power to sue for them.

This is a real (*verum*) dominium, real but not full (*plenum*), and yet less full than the dominium discussed above; for that power is appended to a yet more onerous obligation: one of law. The laity can put any law (*legem*) they please upon goods when they pass over the dominium of them (*traditione*) to the church, as long as it is not contrary to law (*legibus*). To place these requirements (*leges*) not only seems contrary to no laws (*leges*); but even more, no just laws (*leges*) seem able to disenable them (*rebrobari*). So, if they are blocked, their donors can then sue for them (77: 330–45).

Thus, when the pope disbanded the Knight Templar, and tried to give their property to the Knights Hospitaler, many of their protectors (*patroni*, *fundatores*) withstood it and bestowed them (*devoluta*) upon the donors' successors, on the ground that they were given for the defence of the faith, not for the care of the sick (77: 88–96, 118–40).[21]

Another way of stating the same obligatory limit is that the pope has not only a real but a full dominium of power to turn such goods *ad quoscumque usus* as they were given. And even when no specified use is stated, this is the only sense in which the pope acquires "full" dominium: a ministerial sense (77:352–55). For, then, he acquires the dominium as though the goods were ones given to the faithful in common. The will of the donors, unless otherwise expressed, is that their goods be used (*hoc fiat de rebus illis*) for what benefits the beneficiaries and what the church orders (77: 140–68), with a strong conjunction.

Thus, goods held by the church for the friars put the heaviest onus on the owners. For the pope would sin mortally by using goods against donors' wishes, according to the Church Fathers, as by engaging in patronage. More, he would thereby give cause for the faithful sincerely to judge that he was in sin (77: 353–67) and so, as the polemics develop, a heretic and no pope, thus disrupting the faith.

The counterpart to this heaviest onus, however, is important to our thesis on the friars' English uses. For while we have seen that their lack of suit reproduces their position as beneficiaries before the common pleas, and that their protection only by the donee's moral obligation reflects their protections before the chancerial court, there is a price. Even if they are no richer but only the donee is poorer in dominium because of that obligation, it still compromises the friars. The solution is to leave ownership not with the church but with the laity. For these lay protectors (*patroni, fundatores.*) can expel the friars at will, for no reason at all, and with no fault or sin at all on their part. So the friars are poorer for lacking the dominium which the laity retain in goods the friars use, such as in the houses they inhabit, than for lacking the dominium which the church keeps in others of the goods they use (77: 174–89). That is, for living like not continental but English friars, whose houses the seculars and the cities owned, as we saw at the start.

Continuing, however, the law of their ownership rather than its most virtuous settlement, the friars can have not only an objective protection, but also a way to set it in motion, to "trigger" the protective process. Not fully have it; for this option is intuitively sensed to be an essential dimension of rights, as it explicitly and commonly is acknowledged to be in rights discourse today, over and above merely imposed benefits.[22] While the friars could not by any interposed person *(cuiuscumque alius nomine)* resist or bother an owner who expels them (77. 89–99), this is only if done under their own or their order's authority (*nomine proprio vel sui collegii*). (77: 219–26).

However, in addition to their license to use goods, they may also hold another license quite separate from the first, a special license to deal with them at law, even to sell or sue for them (77: 395–405).

One model for this is a servant's pecuniary transactions for his master. A master can allow, even command, a servant to do what otherwise he had no power to do; as Christ by special dispensation could allow an Apostle to deal in money (94: 353–57). Such a transaction is the servant's act; he performs the sale, or he truly buys, he does use the money this way, and not the master. But he performs his own act in the name of another (30: 22, 322 84, 130).

One reason why this can serve as a model is that money has for Ockham, as for all economic thinkers caught in the Roman trap, the ambiguous nature of a sign-value: more indestructible than an immoveable, its dominium transfers with every change of hands more mercurially than the most fully moveable or even consumable (3: 256–320).[23] This is also why the initially promising model does not work, of the Apostles' ladyfriends through whose services the Apostles received goods neither themselves nor by an interposed person (*interpositam personam*), but in such a middling way (*quodam modo mediante*). (6: 95–100) It does not work because, under special license to sue, the friars would be comparable not to the Apostles, but to the ladies.

An alternative model for the special-license "trigger" is the suit for what is in common dominium, not of oneself and his order, but of all the faithful among whom the order's members are to be found as are Christ and the Apostles as well (94: 210–30, 270–80). Here one sues in the name of the whole community for what is common to the whole community (106: 85) and for which, therefore, one might even say, he holds *aliquale dominium* (94: 270–74). However, then the recovered goods are in a "common" dominium only in the sense that they are *communicandum* (88: 33C)–35), a sense which returns us to the moral onus upon owners to foster the intended uses.

What has emerged from this investigation is the following:

A. Ockham has described a set of features for the friars' holdings.
1. The beneficiary has no right to sue for his use, but has only a license.
2. The holder of dominium, when a donee, is under moral obligation to provide use, which has condign consequences when violated.
3. The holder is under no such obligation when he is not a donee, but is a donor.
4. The donor has the right to sue for the provision of this use.
5. The beneficiary can have special license from the holder or the donor so to sue.

B. There is little basis for this mode of holding in Roman continental, civilian property law.
1. Any user has the right to sue for his use, as well as to engage in many other legal acts involving it.
2. A donee-owner has also a legal obligation to provide this.
3. So does a simple owner.
4. The donor has no room to sue for the user, since that one carries suit himself.
5. Still, any principal can mandate any mandatory.

C. There is ample basis for this mode of holding in the English property law which Ockham may well have lived under, and whose development he could desire.
1. The cestui que use has no suit for his uses before the courts of common law.
2. The feoffee to uses has a moral obligation to provide them; failure to do that can be pursued before the courts of chancery with personal punishment.
3. The lay holder or donor, however, can recover his uses at will.

4. The feoffor can seek common recovery only if seisin is not delivered to the feoffee; but recovery for failure to provide the uses can be sought constantly both for him and for the cestui que use.
5. Again, agency can be placed upon any person.

D. Ockham is trying to make more broadly available to his order the legal system which alone has the resources to legitimate or make legal sense of their mode of property holding.

E. These results are the first step of a more demanding research effort.
1. In addition to correction in their own right, they also demand: investigation in Ockham's other writings.
2. The same investigation of the other English friar-philosophers or fellow travellers, and perhaps others; from Marsh through Grosseteste, Bacon and Pechham, perhaps Hales, Bonaventure and Scotus, to such later writers as Marston and Kilwardby.
3. Attempts to discover philosophically and jurisprudentially similar ground in the myriad pamphlets of the poverty debate through two centuries.
4. Searches of administrative materials for reflections by English superiors upon their modes of holding.. e.g., correspondence to and from each other, or with their continental counterparts, and the papacy; deeds of use; explanations to chapters.
5. Searches of judicial materials, as in the records of chancery, for friars' engagements therein.

That verification belongs to an Atlas on the best of days, a Hercules on most, and perhaps a Sisyphus at the end. This chapter hopefully will fall into their hands.

NOTES

1. F.W. Maitland, *Collected Papers*, ed. H.A.L.Fisher (Cambridge University Press, 1911) 408; also in F. Pollock and F.W. Maitland, *The History of English Law Before the Time of Edward I*, 2 ed. (Cambridge, 1923) 231.

2. Thomas de Eceleston, *Liber de adventu minorum in Angliam* (c.1260), in *Monumenta franciscana*, vol. 1 of *Rerum britanicarum medii aevi scriptores*, ed. J.S. Breuer (London: Longman, 1858).

3. On differences from Roman law: Pollock and Maitland 228–33; A. Badre, *Le developpement historique des "uses" jusqu'à l'introduction du trust en droit anglais* (Paris: Rousseau, 1932) 17–24; T.F.T. Plucknett, *A Concise History of the Common Law*, 4 ed. rev. (London: Butterworths, 1948) 544–45. Henceforward, while key terms in Latin will be italicized, and explanatory phrases quoted, the term "dominium" remains in regular print due to its frequent repetition later in the text.

4. On differences from Germanic law: O.W. Holmes Jr., "Early English Equity," *Law Quarterly Review* 2 (1885) 162–70; Badre 24–30.

5. Early deeds are collected in: Maitland 409–14; Pollock and Maitland 233–35.

6. Maitland 409–14; Pollock and Maitland 233–35.

7. Friars' deeds are collected in: Eccleston 16–17; *Prima fundatio fratrum. minorum Londiniae*, in *Monumenta franciscana* 495–509; Pollock and Maitland 414–15; Badre 38–41, esp. p.40, n.l; John Sever, *The English Friars under Henry III* (Oxford: Blackwell, 1940) 52–59; Arthur G. Little, *The Greyfriars at Oxford* (Manchester University Press, 1892) 13–21, 295–307, 315–19; J.B. Ames, *Lectures on Legal History* (Harvard University Press, 1918) 236, n-5.

8. The succinct history that follows can be expanded beyond the standard doctrine of e.g., G.W. Keeton, *The Law of Trusts*, 9 ed. (London: Pitman, 1968) 19–31, by reference first to the expanded histories of a Badre, Ames or Plucknett 546–55; then Anthony Highmore, *The_History of Mortmain*, 2 ed. (London: Butterworth, 1808), and Arthur Hobhouse, *The Dead Hand* (London: Chatto and Windus, 1880); and finally the more recent scholarship of: Olin Brouder Jr., "Trusts and the Doctrine of Estates." *Michigan Law Review* 42 (1974) 1506–76; J.H. Baker, "The Use Upon a Use in Equity 1558–1625," *Law-Quarterly Review* 93(1977) 33–38; E.W. Ives, "The Genesis of the Statute of Uses," *English Historical Review* 125 (1967) 672–97; Desmond H. Brown, "Historical Perspective on the Statute of Uses," *Manitoba Law Journal* 9 (1979) 409–33; J.L. Barton, "The Medieval Use," *Law Quarterly Review* 81 (1965) 562–77.

9. Michel Villey, "La génèse du droit subjectif chez Guillaume d'Occam." *Archives de philosophie du droit* 9 (1964) 97–127 at pp. 117–18.

10. There is a paradox in that the received view of Villey holds Ockham's main contribution in his polemics to be the introduction of the notion of rights. By this he means moral entitlements which inhere in individuals' capacities, the contemporary sense of "subjective rights"; this is distinct from rights as moral obligations which attach to human relationships, the classical sense of "objective rights". Ockham could hardly have meant to exclude objective rights, because this would have run counter to the purpose of his argument, if correctly identified here.

11. Ockham, *Opus Nonaginta Dierum* in *Opera Politica*, vol.1, 2 ed., H.S. Offler (Manchester University Press, 1974), vol.2, ed. J.G. Sikes, H.S. Offler (Manchester, 1963), (OP II). Citation is made of this henceforward in the body of the text, by chapter and lines, to avoid proliferation of footnotes. This is the only text used, for no advance is made on the argument in the books against John and Benedict and no treatment of legal questions on property rather than the scriptural questions on power in the *Breviloquium*.

12. Editors note this as from *Institutes* 2, 5, 1.

13. Editors note this as from the commentator Azo on Digest 7, 8, 1.

14. In this case, at *Institutes* 2, 5, 1, as the editor's note.

15. Ockham's *impugnatores*, however, elsewhere deny that this can be a positive human right *ex constitutiones aliqua vel humana pactione* (61: 47–50). They also deny it arises *ex gratia*, elsewhere (2: 170–79). On the voice-address rhetoric of *impugnati* and the various *impugnatores*, see Preface: 20–22, and 124: 460–66.

16. See the end of preceding note.

17. Ockham first has to show that the subject, the content and the object of an act of using are even possible, all of which John denied. It is in doing this that more recognizably philosophical propositions appear, on universals (62:205–25; 6: 425–55) and on successives (67: 170–255; 73: 20–56). But they are not germane to the present study.

18. Editors note this as from Codex 4, 35, 21.

19. Including the continent, and also England until free testation was permitted as a recompense for making uses futile two centuries later.

20. One of the errors in the *Tractatus contra Benedictum*, in *Opera politica*, vol-3, ed. H.S. Offler. (Manchester, 1956) V, 182: 20–22.

21. "... *English* lay patrons were certainly reluctant to give effect to this decree" as the editors quote A.M. Leys at 77: 133–40, note; my emphasis.

22. E.g., H.L.A. Hart, "Bentham on Legal Rights," in *Oxford Essays in Jurisprudence*, 2d series, ed. A.W.B. Simpson (Oxford: Clarendon, 1973) 171–201.

23. E.g., John Locke *An Essay Concerning the True Original, Extent, and End of Civil Government*, in *Two Treatises of Government*, ed. P.L. Laslett (Cambridge, 1960), para. 37.

CHAPTER ELEVEN

LAS CASAS' MEDIEVAL IDEOLOGY

> Todas las cuales gentes son ánimas racionales, criados y formados en la imagen y simejanza de la Altisima Trinidad[1]

Still today American first nations suffer violence. Much of their property and self-governance remain suspended; their persons are still less likely than others to survive. At some points in this hemisphere, they are subject to renewed attack and exploitation.

Coexistence was achieved in much of this hemisphere, however, by the deeds and designs of Spanish friars, a half millennium ago at the end of the middle ages. The rest of the hemisphere was colonized English, French and Dutch, and lacked such protectors; but the North was indirectly their beneficiaries. The "Black Legend" of Spanish conquistadors' uniquely horrifying cruelty toward Indians kept other colonizers from intruding upon Spain's turf (Saint Lu).

But that the black deeds became a legend at all, that they were even of concern and were discussed, makes up the "Golden Legend" of Spain's search for justice in the colonizing of America. Spain was the only colonizer to whose Crown and Church the violence against Indians was even an issue. This was the only empire which constantly checked its conduct in order to ensure that it remained morally just and legally right. Vocation had to be the motive for its intrusions even when it wasn't; philosophy, theology and international law must justify its actions even when they couldn't.

Friar Bartholomé de las Casas was one principal player in the legends, publicizing the black deeds of violence, resisting their occurrence and presenting a golden alternative. The Dominican of "medieval ideology" (Pidal, a negative critic) set the doctrine for one classic defence of Amerindians against their subjection and deprivation, by adopting medieval doctrines to this task. He adapted these medieval sources, along with their reliance upon ancient philosophy, as did his opponents. I will describe Las Casas' broadening of medieval doctrines, and will recommend their use upon contemporary problematics.

The youth Las Casas watched Cristobal Colón disembark his Amerindians upon returning to Seville in 1492, and received one of them as a page. After a licentiate in law at Salamanca, Las Casas followed his father and brother to take over the family's estate in Cuba; this "encomienda" was entrusted with evangelization of the Indians on a tract of land in return for the entitlement to their services. Las Casas there became the first priest ordained in New Spain. In 1514 he renounced his estate after reading the thirty-fourth chapter of *Ecclesiastes*, and was appointed Defender of the Indians by the king two years later. In 1523 he entered the Dominican order, and spent half a decade in study at Salamanca. Re-equipped he recommenced his defense, by lobbying the Court during some ten return trips from New Spain, and by attacks on the violence of conquest in some eighty larger writings. As a result, although after the first forty years from contact most conquests were completed, the New Laws in 1542 abolished all Indian servitude; but these were revoked three years later. When made a bishop in Mexico in 1544, Las Casas actively used ecclesiastical sanctions such as withholding absolution in order to ensure that no Indians were held, and that restitution of their property was made. Las Casas resigned his see shortly before his famous public debate with Juan Ginés Sepúlveda ordered by the king at Valladolid in Spain during 1550–51 before fourteen jurists, theologians and administrators, on whether war could justly be waged against the Indians: "Utrum barbaris novi orbis, quos Indios hispana consuetudine vocat, liceat bellum inferre". After this concluded, the judges never gave a decision, although Las Casas managed to block publication of his opponent's books in Spain. Las Casas attempted one more colony, where he exercised his convictions on the peaceful preaching to Indians, before returning to Spain. Even then, until dying in 1566 at the age of ninety-two in Madrid, he continued acting for confreres brought by Councils or Inquisitions to answer for views similar to his own, on the lack of authority in Crown or Church to permit violence on the Indians.

Las Casas and his Dominican order were not the only players in the Spanish legend. While the Jeromite monks stood firmly behind conquest and the encomiendas, the Franciscan order shared the Dominicans' stand against violence toward Indians in many respects. Franciscans were less opposed to making war on Indians for the sake of conversion, since even more than Dominicans did they envisage a utopia of Indians living more free from European commerce in their new faith than they had even as animists. Usually these differences did not impede cooperation. Las Casas had worked well with the Franciscan bishops Cisernos and Zumarraga. But in the mid-1550s Las Casas succeeded in obtaining a Crown directive that baptisms could not be celebrated without significant prior instructions. This directive brought a fierce condemnation of Las Casas by his Franciscan counterpart among the apostles of the New World, friar Toribio de Benevente called Motolinia or "the poor man" in Indian. The attack on both

Las Casas' litigious bent as well as his doctrine brought to a head these orders' alternative visions of the New World and its inhabitants.

The reasons for attending to difference among the friars, in regard to their catechetical theology and its relation to violence toward the Indians, is that this allows an entry into an aspect of coexistence with the Indians that is more related to philosophical anthropology and so is available for wider consumption. The debate at Valladolid over the natural slavery of the Indians put Aristotle and the Amerinds into surprising conjunction.

Sepúlveda brought out this Aristotelean theme as was expected of him as one of the foremost Renaissance humanists of the century. Sepúlveda was the translator for one of the six different translations of Aristotle's *Politics* that appeared during the sixteenth century. A tacit participant in the debate was Erasmus of Rotterdam whose Christian pacifism struck the Italian humanists as too close to Luther's doctrine to be tolerated, although the two northerners had shown they were unlikely to join each other. To Sepúlveda, Erasmus' general pacifism was the unspoken horizon for Las Casas' specifically Indian pacifism. To this tendency, Aristotle was the best classical antidote.

That the Indians were barbarous, slaves by nature, and thus fit to be enslaved was only one of Sepúlveda's rationales for approving Spanish wars of conquest . The other three were that Spain had been given authority over the New World, that the Indians' sins needed punishing, and that Indians victimized by others needed help. These rationales took up a discussion already in the public space for fifty years regarding the Indians, and since patristic times more generally.

But these three came down to natural slavery. For, first, if the Indians were free men with rulers they had chosen, then neither emperor nor pope could have given authority over them to another nation, said Las Casas. And punishment of their cannibalism and human sacrifice was appropriate for outsiders only if Spain already held authority for some other reason. These deeds, in fact, were part of a religious belief which, unless they were not free men with religious liberty, they were entitled to follow until conversion. Finally, the defense of Indian nations allied to Spain had happened only once, by Cortez against Moctezuma; and there it was a manipulated appeal and response, that is, not an authentically free one.

So the basic issue in the philosophy of freedom, or slavery by nature, intruded as the crucial premise in each of the other juristic or theological rationales for the conquest. Slavery by nature in Aristotle's *Politics* involved the following steps. Men who must be governed by others can have war waged upon them in order to subject them. If men are not self-governing, they must be governed by others. They are not self-governing if either they cannot discern the ends of human life, or the means to it, or else they are too corrupt to act upon their discernment. In either case, this is a deficiency in their intelligence, in their reason. Those who are slaves by nature, and can be attacked, are those who are deficient in reason.

This is the argument which needs explanation of its terms, its logic and its uses in order to gain purchase upon the view of human being which it incorporates and thus the alternative to it at this deepest stratum which the other mendicant order supplied, as a view to coexistence without violence.

In summary, first, Indians cannot be made into *legal* slaves, because war cannot justly be waged upon them. This addresses the criterion developed by medieval canonists, and continued in the political philosophy of Thomas Aquinas, flanked by the Spanish schools, from Isidore of Seville six centuries before Aquinas, to the classical school of international law including Francisco de Vitoria three centuries after. Vitoria was Las Casas' colleague and confrere at Salamanca.

In turn, war cannot be made upon Indians, because they are not *natural* slaves. This runs contrary to the political philosophy of Las Casas' chief opponent in the debates, the Aristotelean scholar and royal chronologer, Juan Ginés Sepúlveda.

Next, the Indians are not natural slaves, because they manifest the features of *rational* nature. This claim uses the metaphysics and psychology made into the sixteenth century's Aristoteleanism by the Università di Padua. There Sepúlveda was educated under the instruction of Alberto Pio and under the patronage of Cajetan or Thomas de Vio, the general of Las Casas' order, Parisian educated on the lines of the Averroist Aristoteleanism inherited from the medieval Paduan professors Siger of Brabant and John of Jandun, and available to Pio at Padua through Pietro Pompanazzi.

Finally, rational nature assures the dignity of Indians, because it is the *image* of their creator. This imagery was developed differently in the natural theologies by the medieval ancestors of Las Casas' Dominicans, and by those of the Franciscans who were their collaborators and competitors in service to the Indians. Las Casas' version reflects toward both of these.

In the debate at Valladolid, both parties used arguments of right such as those just named, and also arguments of fact as to whether the Indians do meet these criteria. For the facts, Las Casas relies on his own thirty years of acquaintance, Sepúlveda relies upon observations by a traveller at the start of the century. For the doctrinal arguments, Sepúlveda relies on Aristotle, the Fathers, and such recent authorities as John Mayr. Las Casas identifies Mayr as the first to apply Aristotle to the Indians while citing Ptolemy, and as the source of Sepúlveda's "poisons" (Zavala 46).[2] Las Casas relies on Aquinas above all, then Augustine and Aristotle, and cites very little from his confreres even Cajetan and Vitoria (Defence xvi) Las Casas uses Aristotle to reply to Sepúlveda's Aristoteleanism, and uses more Aristotle for his own ends, but eventually dismisses him as inadequate for Christians.[3]

LEGAL SLAVES AND WAR

Las Casas accepts that, in principle, there can be just wars (Friede 95) . He does not share Erasmus' Christian pacifism that was Sepúlveda's real target. But neither does Las Casas agree with any of the reasons why, in particular, war upon the Indians is just, as I have sketched out.

As well, Las Casas agrees that from just wars a legal slavery can justly arise. In mankind's original innocence, slavery had no place. But among men of a fallen nature, wars arise, defense is just, combatants forfeit life, and slavery can substitute for taking the lives of losers. This does not yet identify who their masters are, however. Unlike a similar argument used by Pufendorf, Grotius and Thomasius, human law and the law of nations in a fallen state do not simply replace reason and the natural law of innocence. "Human law cannot dispose anything contrary to natural law and divine law" (Pidal 205). God established order among beings by their natures. That natural order obliges them, i.e., imposes upon them a natural *ley y derecho*. Faith does not supplant this, but only completes it (Defence 339). Las Casas makes this natural law more flexible by making it a matter of nature and circumstances. At the same time, he makes an implicit distinction between nature and essence, by saying that the attribution of natural law to beings contributes to establishing the essences proper to such things (Obra 453–4), rather than the other way around.

WAR AND NATURAL SLAVERY

Several grounds which could justify war and, in cases other than the Indians' legal slavery have already been set out. The ground of particular interest is natural slavery, or the need and obligation to be ruled by others because of a defect in reason. Las Casas agrees with this argument in principle, but changes its conditions, meaning and applications. Here the senses of slavery, and of slavery by nature will be set out, and in the next part the details of nature and of their consequences for natural slavery.

That Las Casas agrees with the natural slavery argument is set out in his *Defence of the Indians* (38). Men who cannot govern themselves are called "barbarians" by Aristotle. But the argument cannot work by reversing its terms, by making anyone called a barbarian into someone incapable of self-governance. Instead, Las Casas identifies several sorts of savages: those who use a different language; those who are less advanced in skill; those who are isolated and alienated by choice; and those who are pagans. Only the third sort are the kind of savages to whom he applies Aristotle's argument. To these, Las Casas admits that it does apply.

Next, these men are "slaves" by nature. Aristotle's term was translated *servi* in the Latin used in Spain, and referred to a social institution defined by permanence, total power, and chattel exchange of persons. Such an institution existed also in Rome, where its members were termed *servi*. Medieval Latin used the term, too, but applied it to persons in vassalage, with the privileges attaching to their role and with their personal possessions, which was the only way Christians could be held by Christians, including potential Christians or pagans. Only non-Christian Turks and Moors, Byzantine heretics and Orthodox schismatics ("slavs") could be held as chattels; and for them the Latin term *esclavi*, or *esclavos* in Spanish was used from the ninth century. For a Renaissance humanist like Sepúlveda, however, only the Ciceronian Latin term *servi* was respectable enough to translate Aristotle, for both senses. Thus in his argument natural "slaves" has an ambiguous sense when used of the Indians, who were viewed as potential Christians (Quirk 357ff.).

In addition, the Indian slave had been compared to the Spanish *naboria*, a servant who could not be sold, as early as 1519 (in Zavala 52). In fact, however, what was being disputed was neither this, nor a Spaniard's purchase of a slave held by an Indian; this Las Casas described as so much gentler a treatment, that these slaves could even be said to be more free than persons with original and ascribed rights (Doctrina 106). Instead, the legal slavery supposedly based on natural capacities was the lethal service in mines and plantations which so quickly destroyed the Indians that the stronger, imported negro slaves brought a much higher price.

The sense of "nature", finally, with which Las Casas is said to be working is first nature, while Sepúlveda is said to be working with second nature (Losada 253). Both disputants agree that they are concerned with human beings, men (*hombres*), not animals. Only later did doubts even on this assurance arise, as in 1629 for Benito de Penaloza y Mondragon, to whom it took a pope's declaration to convince him (Zavala 59).

But Losada takes Las Casas to be understanding, incorrectly, that Sepúlveda means by natural slavery that there are different kinds of men, some truly men or *hombres*, and some merely humanoids or *hombrecillos* to use Sepúlveda's term. As he puts it, this would be to take the *condicion natural* of which Sepúlveda speaks to be a quality constituent of their nature, so that the nature of the natural slave consists in the components of animality plus rationality plus subjection, for example. This constitutes their first nature.

Instead, for Losada, what Sepúlveda meant is that the Indians are backward, but perfectible. Their defects arose from their situation, in particular from their geography and inhospitable climates. This explanation evokes the past astral version of the doctrine, by its mention of John Mayr's citing Ptolemy; and, as the astral gave way to the geographical, so too there are phrasings which anticipate both of these giving way to today's purely cultural version. In any form, it is not first nature, but second nature, men's resultant habits and ways of life, that are their natural slavery. It is their "affections", which shortly loom so large in European thought (Losada 253).

It is unlikely that Las Casas was mistaken about what Sepúlveda was arguing. Las Casas agreed that some beings could be men, but strangers to reason; and that they could be so estranged not only because of evil character, but also because of the barrenness of their region (Defence 32). God conceded power over created things to "the species of human nature"; that is, the biological species is the locus for those substances whose first nature is to be human. And some of them fail. With barbarians in the strict sense, we ought to apply Aristotle's natural slavery, and they ought to be governed by the wiser, for they are natural slaves since they are far from the best in human nature (Defence 38), although they do not lack it. All of these normative expressions are Las Casas'. With such admissions, and with the argument he will actually make, Las Casas and Sepúlveda are not talking at cross purposes, if Losada is right about Sepúlveda.

Thus Las Casas did not deny that humans might be natural slaves. He did give factual evidence from his experience that, if any were, the Indians were not. Las Casas relies much more strongly, however, upon the dynamic of nature, the same as is found in the natural slavery argument, to show that the Indians cannot be natural slaves, whatever their conduct may be, and even though some of them may be.

Aristotelean nature, rational or otherwise, has the dynamic that nature realizes the fulfilled version of its kind, always or for the most part, or at least strives to. Las Casas makes the four selections from Aristotle's opuscula (Defence 34): "Nature always follows the best course possible", "Nature lavishes greater care on nobler things", "Nature makes the best of possible things", "Things which happen by nature have a fixed and intrinsic cause, since they occur uniformly, either always or in most cases". In a fifth paraphrase, Las Casas makes a typical merger between the ensemble of objects, the identifying features of each, and its dynamic toward perfection: "for the most part nature brings forth and produces what is best and perfect. Rarely do natural causes fail to produce the effects which follow from their natures". What the perfection consists in, whose dynamic Las Casas has just portrayed out of Aristotle, is that from any individual there are generated con-specifics, called "likenesses" (Ib.). This final citation, from the Platonist *Liber de Causis* attributed to Aristotle, moves in a different direction, to be identified shortly.

The conclusion is that nature cannot fail in what is necessary to it. This can be interpreted into several directions. It can mean that if something needs to be ruled, it will be ruled (Zavala 48, citing Thomas, Giles and Vitoria). It can also mean what Las Casas took it to mean, that each created thing is owed by nature what is ordered to it, and cannot fail to achieve that (Obra 453). Deficiency can occur, but not much, and rarely (Zavala 77). Only very rarely can freaks appear, those which do not fit the common nature (Defence 35).

Yet a more Platonist direction in which this principle can go is that nature, taken now no longer in the sense of the regular properties of any generable species, but in the sense of the ensemble of these, also obeys the same principle. This nature realizes its perfection in the generation of rational beings. "We are in a way the end of all things", says Las Casas, referring to "The Philosopher" but citing only St. Thomas (Obra 453).

Human nature, as descended from one parent, is a single unity (Gandia 63), and because of its origin in an act of creation it normally will show only rational beings (Zavala 82). Thus, in fewer cases even than among beings of a non-rational nature will nature fail among humans (Defence 35).

The conclusion from stacking the enhanced dynamic of rational nature atop the already perfection-bound dynamic of all natures is that it becomes incoherent and impossible to speak of nature failing in large measure. This it would do if it were to leave an entire people in the condition of natural slaves, those who fail to meet their nature's demands.

Even though Las Casas has by this already countered the application of natural slavery to Indians as a group, his rebuttal continues. For the chief move in Sepúlveda's argument is to locate natural slavery among a list of natural orders, each of which has the binding force of natural law: "Those who are barbaric and sunk in vice are held by natural law to submit to the wise, as matter yields to form, body to soul, sense to reason, animals to humans, women to men, children to adults, the imperfect to the more perfect, the worse to the better, the cheaper to the more precious", "the cruel to the kind, the prodigal to the temperate, and apes to men, all this to the advantage of both" (Defence 12, Pidal 205).

Las Casas plucks from this list the first three—body/soul, sense/reason, and especially the relation of matter to form which supplies the metaphysical fuel for the "yielding" to be found in the several social relationships. In one passage on essence (Obra 454), an Avicennian discourse as infrequent for Las Casas as for his Averroist opponents, Las Casas speaks of matter and form as existing because of the essence of the thing, as constituting that essence, and as contributing to its perfection, and thus to its conservation. Las Casas illustrates this function of the essence's contributing to the perfection of a thing by a mixed bag of examples: a man having hands, the lower animals serving man, and generally the natural *ley y derecho* establishing the proper essence of something. Returning to his usual discourse about nature, the covering principle here is that each created thing is owed by nature what is ordered to it.

Amplifying Las Casas here, this is why the matter is dominated by its form: the form elicits from the potentiality of matter whatever are the demands for completion which the form makes. While it is justly observed that his Averroist opponents do not have room for the potentiality of matter to receive the further forms which adaptation to grace supplies (Pollini), and neither does Las Casas' metaphysical frame, it is also clear that he does not violate the principle that the form cannot be received beyond the potentiality of matter. Las Casas admits, as we have seen, that there are degenerate cases. But he does not make this failure into a characterization of the species.

Whatever the relation of matter to form, however, Las Casas' main rebuttal is his denial that any relation can be drawn out, between matter and form on the one hand, with Indians and Spaniards on the other. While it is correct that the lower serves the higher, and ought to do so, this is so only when the two are joined by nature in first act. (It is hard to say whether nature, here, means the ensemble of generative processes, or the identifying features of a reproducing kind.) When the lower and the higher are separated, however, and exist in different subjects, then the imperfect does not serve the more perfect. In sum, Aristotle is interpreted in the rest of his list to mean only that some are better fitted to rule than others (Defence 48). While there is a normative element to this relation, it is merely evaluative, and not imperative. The relation of matter and form which are constitutive within the substances of a given nature, are not the dynamics which obtain among distinct beings of the same nature, or between several natures. These, too, are ordered; but not as matter and form are. Here, too, there is rule; but there is not the domination which form brings over matter. Las Casas recognizes the difference between first act, and "second nature"; and he sees that his opponents do, too. But his rebuttal takes their smooth set of orderings to show that they do, in practice, blur the distinction and treat beings in first act as though they were related as are the material and the formal components of the nature which, instead, characterizes each one of them.

Natural Slavery and Rational Nature

It is a commonplace that it is rational nature or the deficiency in it which distinguishes the natural master and the natural slave. The reason for this is, of course, that reasoning is the distinctive capacity of rational nature, and reasoning is the capacity to relate likenesses, thereby to set means to ends, and to bring things to their ends, especially the rational nature's own completion and perfection. Las Casas accepts this commonplace along with its rationale. Intellect is how God made men perfect, and standing above all other animals (Defence 35). God disposed as natural law that all things below men are ordered to men's use, and these are subordinated (Obra 453). For this rationale, reasoning must be a skill innate in the soul (Zavala 84), and not merely the capacity to learn which characterizes a *tabula rasa*. (This was the most, that the forementioned Benito could accept as the "first step" of human nature among the Indians, once the Pope had insisted that he recognize them as bearing a rational nature (Zavala 55).) The precondition for reasoning is, instead, shown by all men's knowing of first principles (Defence 35).

Fortunately, however, Las Casas removes himself from such anticipatory Cartesianism, and makes of rational nature instead the nature of such beings as have this reasoning capacity, and not merely an isolated abstraction of that capacity by itself. While that would identify what is most distinctive to beings of a rational nature, such a procedure would be open to rejection: both as undesirable, for dehumanizing a human attribute; as unrealistic, for ignoring the concrete difference which humans have from others; and as theoretically unsound, since the nature of beings is not simply their peak attribute but the complex of their generable properties.

So Las Casas continues that it is as impossible for the majority of men, or for a group of men such as the Indians, to fail in their internal senses as in their ruling reason, because these internal senses serve the highest faculties (Defence 38). As well, the "three very noble highest faculties" include not only the rational, but also the concupiscible and the irascible (Defence 74). Las Casas applies the adjectives only to faculties, and does not characterize these as affects or appetites as distinct from cognitions. Already, however, we have seen that the "affections" or the ways of life which men habitually accept and which are suited to human beings (Defence 33), go to make up human nature. Social attributes are not only the precipitate of reasoning, but are as much its governor as it is theirs. In turn, operative capacities do the same: the mechanical arts scorned by his opponents are evidenced among the Indians as reflecting right reason (Defence 44). Finally, if even in their bodies most men were freaks, again nature would lack its best parts (Defence 3738), which in this case means rational nature.

With this expansion of the senses in which rational nature provides rule, and its deficiency provides natural slavery, we are better prepared for the expansion of rational nature's components or properties yet one step further, into natural liberty. Natural liberty is related to rational nature, not only to reasoning, so that liberty extends further in rational nature than does reasoning, and perhaps is more fundamental than is reasoning.

Natural liberty is a natural attribute; that is, it is not lost *per se*, by a change in nature, but at most only *per accidens*, by reason of circumstances (Friede 102). Even those who are truly natural slaves in Las Casas' view, because of deficiencies in the features of rational nature already listed, "are not naturally free *except* at home, since they have no one to rule them" (Defence 33; my emphasis). Whatever fascinating glimpses about domestic arrangements this unexplained passage may involve, its main thrust is that even natural slaves are not wholly bereft of natural liberty.

The diction of another passage which again Las Casas explains only slightly suggests that rational nature consists in its being provided for its own sake; that the special way in which it is superior consists in its being provided for its own sake, rather than in its having such features as reasoning ability (Defence 35). If so, these capacities would not be valuable for their end-directedness, but for some other reason, yet to be glimpsed. The "special way" in which rational nature is provided, is that it is the way not only for a species, but for each member of it (Defence 35).

The consequence of this is that no free person is bound to submit, no matter how advantageous this would be for the person (Defence 48). Las Casas does not deny natural slavery, nor does he deny that natural law follows from natural ordering, and is obligatory; rather, he denies that the natural ordering has the imperative character which would be obligatory to any particular master. *Dominium*, by now reunited as both jurisdictional and proprietary as in Roman times (Pennington; see my preceding chapter), is a matter of positive law, not natural; from the law of nations, not divine law; by natural reason, not religious grace. Innocent IV, Thomas, Cajetan and Vitoria are said to agree. While this exorcises the loss of dominion for reasons of sinfulness, which Wycliffe had urged (Zavala 33–35), the position also keeps governors from claiming from the divine creation of human nature the full warrant for subordination which follows upon natural slavery.

Just as civil protection as free vassals of the king may be to the Indians' advantage, but cannot be forced upon them, so too jurisdiction over them for the preaching of the Gospel also exists only in potency, and comes to exist *in actu* only through their voluntary acceptance (Lasada 257). To force civilization upon them is unlawful for anyone but the king, and for him it is lawful only by gentle persuasion to accept a better way of life (Defence 39). Thus, rule is "of no force nor entity" unless it is free and unforced, because it changes the natural liberty of its subjects (Bataillon 211).

The alternative to this metaphysic, in fact, would be policy which is absurd. Not only would the paradox of Palacios Rubinos be in play: that rule over irrational beings follows from their capacity, and rule over rational beings follows from their capture; so if infidels obey, they suffer natural slavery, and if they resist, they suffer legal slavery. Even without an equally facile reversal of the paradox, Las Casas had blocked its publication after it was presented at the Junta of Burgos in 1512, an anticipation of his dispute with Sepúveda at the Junta of Valladolid in 1550 (Zavala 47–49). More than this, the legal implementation of natural slavery delegitimates itself. That one people could rise against another upon the pretext of superior wisdom—and in each one's own view of its "superiority", the others are deficient—is an absurd policy: for then any people could do so at any time, confusing all social life, contrary to eternal law, and standing as an act contrary to wisdom, although taken in the name of superior wisdom (Defence 47).

Rational Nature and Image

Las Casas acknowledged legal slavery, and also the just wars from which it would follow; but he denied that such war could be waged on Indians. He admitted of natural slavery, as rare among Indians as among others; but he denied that this was any ground for violating natural liberty. All of this, however, could readily be acknowledged, without providing an ideological protection for the Indians. These facts of their nature are, simply as such, only part of their natural history, and have no more or less imperative force than the natural history that bears hibernate in winter. It is something to be taken into consideration, more or less, perhaps more for rational nature than for others; but it is not overriding nor imperative by reason of natural law. What is needed is a dignity that cannot be overridden, over and above a value which can.

There is already some sense of dignity to human nature, as well as value to it, in the source of natural liberty, namely, that it is for its own sake. But this is both too anachronistically kantian to employ in explaining Las Casas, as well as useless in the longer run, where this, too, is but a self-contained feature of the nature. Las Casas is not an innovator, in supplementing this dignity by the unassailable dignity of human nature's imaging of divine creative existence; but he does it differently, with differences that point toward the several medieval developments, not only of Aristotelean nature as we have seen, but of men and women as image of God.

Rational nature, after the angelic, is nobler because of its "greater resemblance" to God. This is unremarkable, if nonetheless a good factual starting point, except for the fact that Las Casas applies this greater resemblance also to human bodiliness, passions and senses, which as we have seen are features of the rational nature in his descriptions (e.g., Defence 37–38). This factual base has a causal source, which feeds into Las Casas' defence, as well: the nature of man is the same across all men, because there is no more a natural difference among men, than there is one in their creation (Defence 272). While this is an aprioristic unity of the species, as Zavala says (83), it is not the aprioristic rationalism he identifies, for it is not the source of creation alone that is the same, but the way of creation, namely, in a rational nature that is more than reason.

Besides the factual and the causal basis for imagery, there is a consequence from it: "in rational nature, Wisdom shines more". This is because beings of a rational nature are works of Intellect (Defence 35). In turn, this has made humans capable of God, and thus more fully and consequentially God's image. Men, who are naturally rational because of generating conspecific rational likenesses (Defence 34), are made to God's image by being made capable of God; this is why, again, not only the reasoning but the concupiscible and the irascible faculties go into making up rational nature, for it is by these that men are capable of God (Defence 74). The knowledge and desire for God are implanted according to his likeness, not according as he is; and nothing is known or desired except insofar as it bears a likeness (Defence 131). That is, the capacity for God and the likeness of God are mutually implicative. The rational nature, even in the expanded sense Las Casas gives it, is but the appendage to this dynamic, however definitional of God's likeness the rational nature may be.

Capacity for God is what protects even that rare natural slave from legal enslavement, even more than his natural liberty does. "Dominion is based in the image of God; but man is image by his rational nature, not lost by sin", said Vitoria (Zavala 33) against Wycliffe and Mayr. Beyond Vitoria, Las Casas preserves humans' dominion of themselves, individually and collectively, not only from loss by sin, but from loss by deficiency of rational nature, i.e., from defect of governing reason. Capacity for faith is compatible with some natural slavery (Zavala 73, citing Bernardino de Mesa at the 1512 Junta of Burgos), but not with the legal slavery alleged to be available as a result of war upon the few natural slaves. Even if barbarians in the proper sense, they are still created in God's image, not so forsaken as to be incapable of God's kingdom. So they have the right to be treated with kindness, and we owe that to them (Defence 39), rather than we having the right to treat them with war, and they the obligation to submit in natural slavery or to be subjected into legal slavery.

Images and Orders

Las Casas provides the stamp of dignity and protection by reference to capacity and creation. This is fully in line with Aquinas and the Dominican tradition on the image of God. The only treatment of image in Aquinas (*S.Th.* 1, 93, esp. a.6) answers whether there is an image of God in nature. To this, Thomas answers, yes: the image of God is human reason. What this images is the one God, in all its creative imagination, caring providence and goaled foresight. This is the God whom persons know from knowing reason; this is the surety for the dignity of reason, and of rational nature.

There is another image, however, beyond this *vestigium* as Franciscans call it (and Thomas, too: 1 *Sent*. 3, 1, c; *S. C. G.* 1, 8; IV, 26). This is the *imago*, the image of the triune God, not only of the one God. "Todas las cuales gentes son animas racionales, criados y formados en la imagen y simejanza de la Altisima Trinidad" (Doctrina x). This is still most fully achieved in the structure of the soul, says Bonaventure (1 Sent. 3, 2, esp. a. 1, q. 2–3); it is an object of natural theology, I argue in an earlier chapter. But it is not achieved solely in reason. Being more structural, it is even less liable to empirical disconfirmation in the singular case, and a fortiori in the collective case, for lack of evidence. Being communal, it is an image for the respect which such dignity induces interpersonally, even more immediately than the discursive process. It moves from what individual reason is, to what implication that has for the ways humans treat each other.

The Franciscan order shared the Dominicans' stand against violence toward the Indians in many respects, unlike some other orders. But several factors intervened to separate them. Because all who could even desire the faith were capable of it, as was confirmed by the 1537 papal bull, baptisms of large numbers of Indians after very brief catechesis was possible. The Joachimite millenarism of the Franciscan Spirituals urged this upon them; it was important to obtain the largest number of conversions in the short time which remained. Mass conversion, in turn, was not incompatible with armed intervention, which could first subject Indians, and then proceed to convert them in large numbers more effectively. Las Casas' main problem with this, was that the conflict alienated the Indians from such conversion.

Slow catechesis and the Dominicans' defence of the Indians, on the other hand, were as tightly connected as the Franciscans' quick conversion and armed intrusion. An essential part of Las Casas' defence of the Indians against the argument that Spain had the right and a duty to subvert in order to convert, was that adherence in faith is an act of freedom. Faith requires free adherence; this required, that the intellect be properly informed. Providing such a formation is more time consuming than the affective appeal to the Indians' desire for conversion used by the Lesser Brothers.

There is irony in Las Casas' catechetical distance from the Friars Minor, while his activism relied on an argument from imagery more akin to their tradition. Las Casas' devoted reliance upon his confrere Aquinas was ambiguous; and his contemporary confrere Vitoria's positions were as often on Sepúlveda's side as upon Las Casas' (Pidal 130–34, Losada 269–79). Gandia's attribution to Las Casas of the position as a continuator of St. Francis, for preaching to all the men on earth, recapitulates the ambiguity (Gandia 133).

Equally ambiguous is the outcome. The Royal Order of 1530 prohibited Indian slaves; but in 1534 it was modified. The Papal Bull of 1537 excommunicated slavers; but it was not promulgated. The New Laws of 1540 redesigned the plantation system; but they were repealed in 1544. A Council Order ended new conquests in 1549; but they continued. The King during Las Casas' post-Junta career refused in 1560 a wide attribution of rights to him over the New World; but the Minorites were the ones still urging these upon him.

The struggle remained to be carried on anew; but no struggle would even have been ongoing but for interventions like Las Casas' upon each of these events. If it is illuminating to know of Vaclav Havel's affinity to phenomenology in view of his role in the Czech liberation, or that Ed Broadbent is a Mill scholar considering his former leadership of the major Canadian social-democratic party, all the more relevant is it to grasp the medieval ideology of Las Casas, as a key player, at the only time in history when a government suspended its war in progress in order to determine its moral uprightness. No such heroic gesture as Spain's is needed, in order for our nation states to complete the just dealing with our first peoples, whether separated in the "two-row wampum" favored by the Franciscans, or self-governing under state protection in the ideology of Las Casas.

References

Bataillon, Marcel, André Saint-Lu. *El padre Las Casas y la defensa de los Indios*, tr. J. Alfonza, B. McShane. Barcelona: Editorial Ariel, 1976.

Friede, Juan. *Bartolomé de las Casas precursor del anti colonialismo*. Mexico Ediciones Siglo Vienticento, 1974.

Friede, Juan, and Benjamin Keen eds. *Bartolomé de las Casas in History;Toward an Understanding of the Man and his Work*. De Kalb IL: Northern Illinois University Press, 1971.

Gandia, Enrique de. *Francisco de Vitoria el Nuevo Mundo; El problema teologico juridico del hombre americana y de la independencia de America*. Buenos Aires: Ekin, n.d.

Hanke, Lewis. *Aristotle and the American Indians: A Study in Race Prejudice in the Modern World*. Bloomington: Indiana University Press, 1965.

—— *The Spanish Struggle for Justice in the Conquest of America*. Boston: Little, Brown, 1965.

Las Casas, Bartolomé de. *In Defence of the Indians; The Defence . . . Against the Persecutors and Slanderers of the Peoples of the New World Discovered Across the Seas*, tr. ed. C.M. Stafford Poole. De Kalb IL: Northern Illinois University Press, 1974.

Las Casas, Bartomolé. *Doctrina*, 21 ed., ed. Agustin Yánez. Mexico: Edicione de la Universidad Nacional Autonoma, 1951.

Las Casas, Bertolomé. *Obra Indigenista*, ed. Jose Alcina Franch. Madrid: Alianza Editorial, 1985.

Losada, Angel. *Fray Bartolomé de las Casas a la luz de la moderna critica historica*. Madrid: Editorial Tecnas, 1970.

MacNutt, Francis A. *Bartolomé de las Casas: His Life, Apostolate and Writings*. Cleveland OH: Arthur C. Clarke, 1909.

Maldonado, Enrique Ruiz. "Tomás de Aquino, Bartomomé de las Casas y la controversia de Indios," *Studium* (Avila-Madrid) 14 (1974) 519.

Mechoulan, Henri. *L'antihumanisme de J.G. de Sepúlveda; Etude critique du "Democritus Primus"*. Paris: Mouton, 1974.

Mohn-Lot, Marianne. *Bartolomé de las Casas et le droit des Indiens*. Paris: Payot, 1982.

Paul III, *Sublimis Deus*, 1537; in MacNutt, 428–9.

Pennington, Kenneth J., Jr. "Bartolomé de las Casas and the Tradition of Medieval Law," *Church History* 39 (1970) 149.

Pidal, Ramon Menendez. *El padre Las Casas; su doble personalidad*. Madrid: Espana-Calpe, 1963.

Pidal, Ramon Menendez. *El padre Las Casas y Vitoria*. Madrid: Editorial Espana Calpe, 1958.

Pollini, Pierluigi. "Bartolomé de las Casas e J. Ginés Sepúlveda di fronte alla questione della liberta degli indios," *Revista di filosofia neo-scolastica* 74 (1982) 343.

Quirk, Robert E. "Some Notes on a Controversial Controversy: Juan Ginés Supúlveda[sic] and Natural Servitude," *Hispanic American Historical view* 34 (1954) 357.

Sevilla-Casas, Elias. "Notes on Las Casas' Ideological and Political Practice," pp. 15–30, in *Western Expansion and Indigenous Peoples; The Heritage of Las Casas*, ed. E. Sevilla-Casas. Hague: Mouton, 1977.

Yanez-Barnuevol Luis, ed. *En el quinto centenario de Bartolomé de las Casas*. Madrid: Ediciones Cultura Hispanica, Instituto di Cooperacion Iberoamericana, 1986.

Zavala, Silvio. *Filosofia de la Conquista*. Mexico: Fondo di Cultura economica 1947.

NOTES

1. Las Casas, in Yanez x. Unless the text indicates otherwise, references in the text to Las Casas' doctrine by my citation of other authors is a reference to their deployment of those among Las Casas' more significant eighty writings which were less available to me.

2. Zavala's and Las Casas' view of Mayr's influence on Sepúlveda is perhaps as excessive as Mohn-Lot's (76) view that Las Casas' doctrine is entirely taken from Cajetan.

3. Aristotle, *Politics*, I, 2; 4, 1245b, 1253b, 1254a; 5, 1254b, 1255a; 8, 1256b; III, 14, 1285a.

www.ingramcontent.com/pod-product-compliance
Ingram Content Group UK Ltd.
Pitfield, Milton Keynes, MK11 3LW, UK
UKHW012042150926
475560UK00001B/150

9 780761 859208